KAZMAINEA!

An International Adoption Memoir

How our crazy journey from Maine to Kazakhstan
led us to the Good Life we never knew we wanted.

Mike Vayda

Heidi Warren Vayda

ISBN: 978-0-9834949-1-1

Printed in the United States of America

This book is dedicated to adoptive parents.
Less than two percent of all orphans are adopted.

It's your love that is changing the world.

We're standing in an airport in Kazakhstan

at midnight with thousands of dollars strapped to our bodies.

The man in the tiny smoke-filled customs office speaks a little English and asks a lot of questions. *Why are you here? Where are you going? How long will you stay?* And then, scariest of all, *Are you carrying any US currency?*

Of course we're carrying US currency. Twenty thousand dollars, if you must know. Fresh from our bank back in Maine.

Back in Maine, where we seriously wish to be right now.

Cigarette dangling from his lips, he makes a gesture that is universal: *Show me the money!* We take a breath, untuck our shirts, unzip our sweaty money belts, and lay out the contents.

We all stare at the stacks of new bills on the table. This could be the most money this guy has ever seen. Heck, it's the most money *we've* ever seen. What if this man from customs declared he would be keeping it?

Squinting through the smoke, he nods and waves us away like a bad thought. We thank him as though he just gave his kidney and hastily grab the cash and secure our belts. We stumble out into the noisy airport.

The place is chaos. We face a wall of people moving, talking, shouting, smoking, holding signs with strange letters. Dozens of eyes are on us. Our tired brains register an unsettling fact: we are the only Americans in sight. Did they see us leaving the customs office? Do they know why we are here? Do they know what's in our sweaty belts?

We are supposed to meet the guy who will drive us to our apartment. Except, we don't know what he looks like. With eyes burning from the smoke and lack of sleep, we search the faces, looking for...what, exactly? We don't know. The faces look back at us blankly.

Here we are. Two mild-mannered, middle-aged adults from Maine, in an airport in Kazakhstan, in the middle of the night, all alone. No one to call. No one but us. This is crazy!

This is *KazMainea*.

TABLE OF CONTENTS

After this picture, we would never be the same.

This is us, back in 2004, the day we left for Kazakhstan. We knew adopting orphans from a foreign country would change us. But man, we had no idea just how much.

At the time, Mike was happily traveling the world for his business. We had just built a big house. We were talking about retiring early. Because of the journey that began right after this picture, everything changed. And it all started with a blog.

The internet was relatively new and amazing back then. We could send words and pictures from the other side of Earth to our friends and family so they could be part of the journey, too. *KazMainea* was our one connection to all we knew.

In the years since the adoption, friends would say, "Hey, that *KazMainea* blog? You guys should make it into a book!" We agreed and, over the years, we began many times. Life always got in the way, though. Raising five children does that. But the desire to tell the story was never far from our minds.

Finally, with Nik and Meg close to graduating high school, we determined to make one final push. And a funny thing happened. We realized the blog was just the beginning. There was a lot more to tell.

We began writing this book as a look back at a specific event. We now see that our adoption was more than a trip to a foreign country. It was the beginning of a journey into a new, undiscovered life. The experiences we share in this book changed every part of our lives, forever.

A few years after the adoption, we were traveling the world together, but it wasn't for business. It was for our new nonprofit. Instead of getting closer to financial independence, we were helping others get closer to the Good Life in India, South Africa, South America, and the US.

Turns out, the adoption journey led us into life we always needed. We just didn't know we needed it yet.

We didn't know a lot of things when we smiled for the camera. Probably a good thing! Ahead of us was a scary, funny, crazy global journey with twists and turns and people and food and experiences so different, we couldn't possibly prepare ourselves. But as a result, we got Nik, Meg...and the Good Life.

Welcome to *KazMainea*. We're so glad you're coming along for the ride!

How to read this book

KazMainea follows our adoption journey chronologically. We tell our story in several ways:

Blog Posts

Each chapter begins with our original blog post from 2004. You'll travel right along with us as you read our actual words from the journey, as it happened.

Thoughts from Now

Adding thoughts from today accomplishes three goals:

1. We were told to assume anything we wrote was monitored, so we posted conservatively. We'll tell you the rest of the story, what we couldn't say back then.

2. For most people, adoption, particularly international adoption, is a mystery shrouded in misunderstanding. We'll tell the whole truth here.

3. You'll also read reflections on life we frankly didn't realize until we wrote them for this book. We surprised ourselves!

Transparency

We want to open up the world of adoption, so you'll see our actual documents, instructions, and, yes, the cost.

Tips & Tricks

Along the way, we'll offer you our opinions on travel, food, cultures, adoption and life.

Bonus: Discover the Good Life along with us!

During our journey, we learned what makes life fulfilling. We call them the "Seven Elements," and you'll see some "light bulb" moments throughout the book under the *Good Life* header (the complete list is on page 5).

Also, we've written a few questions at the end of each section. We encourage you to discuss them with a group of friends to get closer to your own Good Life.

THE 7 ELEMENTS OF THE GOOD LIFE

What we learned on our journey.

1. **Own:** Know yourself and what you need.

2. **Be**: Understand others and help them.

3. **Plot**: Map out a plan to create your unique Good Life.

4. **Clarify**: Craft a simplified life where everything…fits.

5. **Amplify**: Expand your Good Life to make it better.

6. **Power**: Plug into a system to live the Good Life daily.

7. **Presence**: Thrive in your uniqueness…the Good Life!

Get closer to *your* Good Life!
For your **free** study guide and more,
go to **NotFar.org/Kaz**

Disclaimer

Each adoption is unique. Opinions are ours alone.

Small changes were made in posts for clarity and grammar.

The quality of the pictures is less than today's standard.

A few names and details have been changed for privacy or because we forgot them.

Part 1

Off you go then...

1. Kazakhstan, Here We Come!

June 1, 2004
Posted by Heidi & Mike

Welcome to KazMainea!
As you may know, in the near future we will be flying to the country of Kazakhstan to adopt two children. You can read about our adventure here in this blog. We're excited to have you join us on this journey!

Who are we? We're a middle-aged couple living in Maine with three children. Zack is eleven, Jake, seven, and our daughter Brynn is six. We are getting ready to complete our family by bringing two children home.

Why the name "KazMainea"?
As soon as I (Mike) knew we were going to do a blog, the first priority was crafting a catchy name. I wanted something brilliant. Something edgy. I finally gave up on that. Instead, I combined a part of the country where we are going (Kaz), where we live (Maine), and our state of mind throughout our process (absolute mania).

"Kazakhstan?! I've never heard of that. Is it a country?"
Yes, it is, and no, don't feel bad that you don't know. Honestly? We had no idea, either. Yet, look at a world map and there it is right in the middle! It's under Russia and a little to the left of China.

So, this country we'd never heard of before will become part of our lives forever. If it all goes according to plan, of course.

Where in this big country are we going? Well, we don't know yet. This is one of the many mysteries awaiting us.

Stay tuned and welcome aboard!

— NOW —

HEIDI: Now Mike and I are beyond middle aged and our children are practically all grown. How time flies!

We were excited about going to Kazakhstan even though we didn't know our exact destination. We enjoy travel and we looked forward to experiencing this new and foreign country.

How did we know what country to adopt from?

First, we found what countries were open to adoption. Kazakhstan was on friendly terms with the US. Good relations were important because a country could close its doors anytime. This is why any negative rumblings from a country were taken seriously. There are many heartbreaking stories of adoptive parents in the process of getting their children when the country suddenly closed its doors and the adoption came to a screeching halt. It's devastating for the parents and the children. We did not want to have that tragedy happen to us. (By the way, even though Kazakhstan is still officially open, no adoptions have taken place for years.)

In a way, Kazakhstan chose us. Each country has its own criteria of who can adopt, the number of children allowed, the age of prospective parents, and more. Kazakhstan was one of the few Asian countries open to parents like us, who already had children by birth and wanted to adopt more than one child.

Also, Kazakhstan allowed parents to visit the orphanage. For me, this was a big deal. I wanted to see firsthand where the children lived. By visiting their "first home," Mike and I would see and experience, in part, the first years of their life. This would give us another way to connect and to bond with our adopted children. Being able to share with them where they began their lives might also give them a deeper connection to their birth country, something they would have no memory of otherwise.

People can't just go to a country by themselves and adopt a child (at least not legally). So, after deciding on a country, we located a Georgia-based agency that worked with Kazakhstan. They would be our guide throughout the journey, leading (and at times, nagging and pushing) us through the hoops and rules and ever-changing guidelines of an international adoption.

```
FINAL DEPARTURE CHECKLIST

Family Name      Vayda              Date to be in Kaz __TBD
Arrival City Almaty      Adoptive city  TBD

          PLEASE READ THIS ENTIRE CHECKLIST CAREFULLY!
The time has come to review everything before you leave for your adoption trip.  You should already know
most of this information, but it is still very important for you to review everything on this list. We have tried to
the best of our abilities to prepare you for everything to expect, but you must remember, international adoption
sometimes has many changes during the process that we have no control over.  This check list is to be referred
to in addition to your program manual, especially the Your Trip to... packet you received after accepting your
referral, please review everything carefully! Read this checklist over and call your coordinator with any
questions you have about any part of your pending trip.
```

Welcome to adoption! This is the beginning of almost 30 pages of instructions from our Georgia agency. Note the unsettling "TBD's."

Next, we found an agency in Maine for our home study. After applications were completed, we began our process by filling out a lengthy form that included over 100 questions!

What is a Home Study?

A home study evaluates you and your living situation, and hopefully approves that you are adoption-worthy. It includes visits to your house, pre- and post-adoption meetings, reports, a home walk-through, reviewing references, and a weekend workshop…to name just a few.

MIKE: *I can see now that KazMainea was more than an adoption trip. It was a journey from the life we knew into a brand new one. It really was an "undiscovered country." It wouldn't be easy to get there, either. There were plenty of obstacles and sacrifices along the way. We had to give up many precious pieces of our old way of living. For me, the first sacrifice it demanded was my beloved privacy.*

I liked living my own life, as I chose. Foolishly, I didn't see any reason why I needed to change that, just for an adoption. (Not very bright, was I?) So when Heidi gave me the home study form, the one with over 100 questions, I made sure I gave as little information as possible.

But as the old song says, I fight authority, authority always wins. The caseworker came to meet with me. I expected a taskmaster. She was surprisingly low-key. She asked me for further clarification on the questions. I kept answering in the same way that I did on the form, with the minimum of personal information.

She put down her pencil and kindly but firmly confronted me.

"Mike, it feels like you're not very keen on being open with me. Is that true?"

I sighed. "Look. I'm feeling like this whole process is one endless intrusion. The questions are too personal. I'm just trying to help two orphans, and I'm being interrogated like I'm a criminal. Frankly, my personal life is none of these peoples' business!"

She slowly nodded. "You're right."

"Huh?"

"Yes, I agree. All I can say is, it's the nature of the beast. In essence, if you want to adopt, you have to play the game. You have to give them what they ask for. Either that, or..."

"Or we can't adopt." I finished her sentence.

I really appreciated her honesty. I still didn't agree, but at least I understood. I needed to swallow my indignation and play by their rules if I wanted this adoption to happen. Like it or not, I needed to share.

I wish I could tell you I got in line and fully accepted the process after that. Instead, I would find myself battling "The Man" throughout the journey. This adoption would demand unquestioned obedience over and over. That is something I don't do well. I'm sure that made it harder for me (and Heidi) than it had to. But at least that honest conversation with the case worker helped me not be quite so belligerent. And the journey could begin.

HEIDI: The weekend workshop proved to be enlightening...and worrisome. We discussed expectations we as adoptive parents might have and difficulties we might face when a child enters the home. It also provided opportunities to troubleshoot scenarios like:

- What if your child was not adjusting?
- What if something was wrong with your child that was not previously known?
- What about negative or inappropriate comments by family, friends and strangers?

The issues raised were eye opening and troubling as it brought to light the many ways an adoption placement can go wrong.

MIKE: *Ah yes. The workshop. Another requirement. More privacy to give up. We were all sitting around in this "sharing circle" and I was, of course, not sharing. The leader was talking about how bringing foreign children into an existing family structure would disrupt* *everything that you know. And, all of a sudden, I realized: Good lord, I'm now a minority family!*

The Good Life: Own

***Own** is the first Element to living the Good Life.*
It means to know yourself & what you need to be happy.
I got this mental image of all of us walking through the mall and two of my five (not three) children would be brown (ish), Asian Kazakhs. It was a shock to the system. I needed to start owning that picture: our family would be different from here on out.

It was disturbing, but it sparked a memory. When I was in high school, my best friend was African American (and he still is.) One day, he took me with him to get his hair cut downtown. At that time, all I ever knew was white, suburban, middle class culture. For the first time in my life, I was a minority. It was an uncomfortable, amazing experience. There's an old saying, something about how a fish doesn't know what air is because swimming in water is all it's ever known. I experienced the "air" of being a minority that day in the barbershop.

Now, because of this adoption, I would be leaving the water I swam in, leaving it forever. It was a splash in the face that I needed.

Now, I could actually picture how my life was going to change. It wasn't an easy thought to accept, but at least I knew what my new life would look like. Multicultural!

The Good Life: Be

***Be** is the second Element to living the Good Life.*
It means to understand others and help them be happy.
All the personality tests tell me I am great with systems, ideas, vision. People? I find them much more of a puzzle. Because of the adoption, I would have the opportunity to see life through different eyes. Adoption took away my order and privacy; it gave me a bigger, better, richer world.

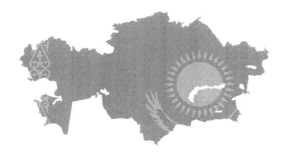

2. The Waiting Is the Hardest Part

June 15, 2004
Posted by Mike

We're still waiting to hear where and when we're going. We joined an online group for parents who are adopting or have adopted from Kazakhstan. It seems many are going to a place called Karaganda, so we're thinking that's where we'll be going. We'll see. Karaganda is in the northeast of Kazakhstan. I'm trying to do some research into that area in preparation.

While we're all waiting, here are a few Kazakh Fun Facts I've learned! (Pay attention: there will be a quiz later.)

1. Kazakhstan is the 9th largest country in the world.
2. But Kazakhstan has a small population, about 16 million.
3. Kazakhstan was part of the USSR until independence in 1991. Now it's a republic.
4. Kazakhstan is home to the Soviet space program. The first man in space left from there.
5. Kazakhstan has huge amounts of natural resources. The superpowers are noticing.
6. Kazakhstan is supposedly the home of apples. I guess they began there. Dunno how.
7. The word "Kazakh" means wanderer. The original people were nomads.
8. Karaganda still has a lot of Russian influence and is an industrial center.

And that's about all I got while we are waiting. Waiting. It's the hardest part, you know. We'll keep you posted!

> Obtaining the invitations is very difficult and very unpredictable due to the number of hands that must actually touch it/approve it. In the past, our partners literally had to walk down the street to a local travel agent to get the invitation; this is no longer the case. Your invitation must now be sent to the Department of Education in the city from which you are adopting by courier, where several individuals review it. Then it is sent by courier again to the Ministry of Foreign Affairs in Astana for several people there to review and sign off on. Then the courier takes it back to Almaty. All of this takes time and due to the number of people involved, there is no way to predict how long any one person will have it on their desk. Our partners go by what they *think* will happen, by what happened the last time. Unfortunately, this does not mean the same timeframe will occur for you! It usually does, but that does not make you feel better when you are in the 5% of the family's

About official invitations, from our agency's documentation.

HEIDI: After nearly a year of research and paperwork, our invitation to adopt came through. Now, there was only one thing left to do. *Wait.* Waiting IS the hardest part. We wondered every minute of every day when we'd get that call saying it was time. Time to get on a plane and travel halfway around the world to bring home the children we dreamed of and worked so hard for.

Why did I want to adopt, anyway?

After all, we already had three wonderful birth children: Zack, Jake and Brynn.

I have always wanted to adopt from an Asian country. During the Vietnam airlifts when I was a child, I remember the grief I felt watching babies being put on helicopters. My parents were hoping to be selected for one of those babies. Partly due to the number of children they already had, they were not approved. I saw my mom in tears, knowing none of those children would become part of our family.

My parents persevered, though, in getting approval from other countries. First came two babies, my new brother and sister from Thailand. Then, came a thirteen-year-old sister from India. After that, a two-year-old brother from here in the US and, last but not least, came a seven-year-old brother from Romania.

So, I have five adopted siblings and seven siblings by birth. This makes me the oldest of thirteen children! I loved being the oldest of a large family and I loved that we looked different from each other. I was fine not being the typical family because, above all, I believed my family made a better life for others and I was determined to do the same.

MIKE: *Why did I want to adopt? Let me tell you a story.*

Unlike Heidi, I had very little experience with adoption. I knew one kid in grade school who was adopted, and he was kind of an odd duck. So my opinion wasn't too positive. That all changed when I was in college.

The year was 1985. I was on my first date with a cute, quiet little blonde I noticed in French class. Here we were, just the two of us, driving in her 1978 Buick. The radio was on. We were deep in conversation. We were only about an hour into our relationship when she boldly announced that anyone who wanted to marry her had to agree to adopt.

HEIDI: We were just getting to know each other and, since we were discussing hopes and dreams, I figured I might as well be upfront about it.

MIKE: *No beating around the bush for her! I had rarely even thought about adoption since grade school. But, suddenly, because of this intriguing young woman, I decided to start.*

And now, as a result of that first conversation, there I was, almost 20 years later, getting ready to launch into a life I'd never imagined.

Throwback: Our wedding day, 9.24.88

3. Taraz?! A Change of Direction

June 20, 2004
Posted by Heidi

The adventure begins! We got the call. A new area in Kazakhstan has recently opened for adoption. It's called Taraz. "Are you interested in going?" they asked.

This place was not even on our list of possibilities; it's that new! After asking for more details, we thought about it and said yes. So, surprise! We are NOT going to Karaganda. We are going to Taraz!

Whereas Karaganda is in the northeast of the country, Taraz is in a remote region of southern Kazakhstan. Mike couldn't find much about Taraz on the internet. It looks awful close to a couple other countries we know nothing about. He said the official website for the city looks like it was created at the dawn of the Web!

After we fly to Kazakhstan, we will have to take an overnight train to get there.

So it seems like it will add quite a bit more travel time, there and back, twice! We have no idea what this train looks like either. A whole lot of mystery, for sure. Exciting, but a little scary, too!

Well, at least we know *where* we're going now. The next big question is, *when*?

Stay tuned! We'll let you know as soon as we do.

HEIDI: In our minds, Karaganda was our destination (since our agency had suggested that might be the place). When we were contacted with this alternative, we were surprised. We were told that, if we chose this new location, our waiting time would likely be shorter. Shorter wait time? "Why, yes, I believe we are interested in this unknown, mysterious place called Taraz!"

We also got the distinct impression that we'd be the first adoptive parents going to this new region so we were a bit nervous.

---

*Expense money -If you are staying the entire 5 weeks in:
Shchuchinsk/Kokshetau - $7000 - 2 trips? $4k on the 1st $3k on the 2nd
Petropavlovsk/Karaganda - $6000 - 2 trips? $3k on the 1st $3k on the 2nd
Akkol/Astana $7000 - 2 trips? $4k on the 1st $3k on the 2nd
Almaty 5 weeks - $5000 - 2 trips? $2k on the 1st $3k on the 2nd
Uralsk - $5000
Almaty (3 weeks), **Essik** or **Taldy Korgan** - $4000

We're Pioneers! Here's the list of cities our agency worked in.
Notice Taraz is not one of them.

MIKE: *There we were, thinking we were heading to Karaganda to adopt two strangers, and suddenly our agency tells us they're sending us to a mystery city to adopt two different strangers!*

I can see now how we shouldn't have planned on Karaganda in the first place. After all, no one actually said we were definitely going there. And, of course, no one was forcing us to go to Taraz.

But it was difficult for me, because it revealed the seeming... randomness of the whole process. Now, we were going to Taraz. It was a completely different destination! And, even more scary, that meant there were two different little strangers who would be my children. It felt like chaos.

Living a life of faith is important to the two of us, even though it's a challenging way to live. For me, this was faith on a whole new level. I had to try to trust that the children we were adopting would be "the ones" for us, regardless of what city they came from. Pretty hard for a practical brain like mine. Another challenge on this journey, right out of the gate. Faith over logic. Not an easy navigation.

Taraz & the Silk Road

Taraz was a key stop on the ancient Silk Road. Wikipedia says the Silk Road "...connected the East and West, and was central to the economic, cultural, political, and religious interactions between these regions." It couldn't be *too* dangerous...could it?

HEIDI: Interesting that Taraz was a historical crossroads for the world. Taraz would be the place where our old life would end and our new life would begin. Two tiny orphans waiting in that baby home were about to come into contact with us. And we were about to travel thousands of miles from our home to meet them. What a fascinating, scary thought that was.

4. We Have Dates!

July 20, 2004
Posted by Mike

Okay, we have dates!

This is a big deal. We've officially been invited to come to the country, so now everything begins to happen. This means that we are indeed going to Kazakhstan to adopt two children. This means that we have a lot of things to do before we leave. This means that we'll be leaving in just two weeks.

This means, yikes.

We are now in the process of getting flights. This feels like the starting gun has fired for our race at last. There's a lot to take into account when trying to find the right flights. They have to fit into our travel dates. They have to be as cheap as possible. It's also helpful to not have a lot of layovers. I'm busy scouring the internet and calling airlines to compare.

Meanwhile, we're starting to pack, and still pulling together necessary documents too.

We will post the itinerary once all is set. It won't be long—whether we're ready or not!

— NOW —

HEIDI: The wait is over. We jumped on the internet to compare the limited options. After a lot of research and phone calls, we were able to use Mike's frequent flyer miles to buy our tickets. It felt great to have our plans finalized.

> *Your immediate task at hand is getting your flights, we will need them ASAP regardless of when you are scheduled to leave. We also need the last page of this checklist completed in full and faxed back to us ASAP. Preferably within FOUR days!*

We always felt like things were being demanded of us in such short schedules. "ASAP" was coming up a lot in our agency emails.

Frequent Flyer Pros and Cons

Fly with one airline group consistently and you collect "miles" that can be exchanged for free flights. But options are limited, making it hard to get flights on the dates you need. (Some of our flight research is to the right.) And if your plans change, you need to start the whole process over again. It felt like a part-time job trying to find that elusive flight. We were thrilled to get tickets all the way to Kaz, free!

After we committed to Taraz, we were sent short videos and brief medical histories of the children. We could not wait to see these children on video! At the same time...did we? What would we think? How would we feel? Would we just know this is right...or not?

In our original application we requested siblings but, as time progressed, it became evident that would mean further waiting. Feelings were tumultuous as we attempted to make the "right" decision. In the end we decided that these two children, the ones we were watching on video, the ones who were extremely small for age three, who were from the same baby home since birth, would be for us.

We felt at peace with the decision...for about two days. Until, that is, we spoke to a pediatrician in Boston who specialized in medical issues of foreign adopted children. I wanted to hear what every parent hopes to hear: "I see no issues here. Your children appear perfectly healthy so, by all means, confidently continue your adoption!"

This is completely unrealistic, of course, but isn't it what we all want to hear? She actually said something like, "Although nothing glaring stands out, I must list for you all the potential medical issues your children could have." She then proceeded to do so. And there were a lot of them!

MIKE: *The doctor said you can never tell for sure what is true when you receive medical records from a foreign country. She kept saying things like, "Could...possibly...potentially." All I heard was the other part, "Fetal Alcohol Syndrome...encephalitis...brain damage...retardation..." After a while, all the words just jumbled together into one big scary unknown.*

HEIDI: I got off the phone reeling. I didn't know what to think. I watched the short VHS tapes of the children over and over until I finally realized that I was looking for some kind of guarantee of health, some kind of certainty. Eventually, I thought, there were no guarantees during my pregnancies. So why would I think there would be a guarantee now? No doctor, no information, no video could provide certainty.

MIKE: *The truth was, we had no idea what diseases or damage these children would have. And yet, we're supposed to say, "Sure! We'll be right over to pick 'em up!"*

How illogical! Could I accept this immense uncertainty? I really didn't know. I felt like I was in a movie, and the best I could do was play a pre-scripted part. "So, these two children on the videos will become my kids? Alrighty, then." Any semblance of control was quickly leaving my life.

Thankfully, I did something smart at this point. Instead of just worrying, I started a routine I would do a thousand times along the way. I shook my head at the absurdity...and prayed. I prayed these kids weren't nearly as bad off as that doctor implied. I wasn't playing my part very well. But at least I was praying.

And this was just the beginning.

5. ~~We Have Dates!~~
We Have *Different* Dates!

July 22, 2004
Posted by Heidi

We thought we had final travel dates. Well, guess what? We spoke too soon. We got an email:

"The Judge in Taraz is going on vacation, so you need to change your dates."

Vacation?!

This means that everything is changing. We had finally found awesome flights...for free! It was really exciting because we were able to use Mike's frequent flyer miles to get the tickets.

Now, we have to start over again. We are scrambling now to change our flights. We may not be able to use frequent flyer miles. This means, it may be costing us a lot more to get over there. And time is running out.

We've got a few other thoughts about this change and what it means to our plans and our mental state. We will keep those to ourselves.

Please be thinking of us as we hopefully get this figured out. Thank you!

– NOW –

Travel dates - I wanted to take a minute to explain a little more about travel dates and potential delays after they have been given to you. First off, your dates are our facilitator's best-case scenario; basically, you will arrive on the given date as long as everything falls into place, on this side of the planet, as well as theirs, so on occasion travel dates can and do change. This is something you need to prepare yourself for, both mentally and financially. Fortunately changes in travel dates are few, but the reasons why they would change are many. The

From our agency's information. Can't say they didn't warn us.

MIKE: So frustrating! I was onsite with a client when I read the email about the judge going on vacation. It was a hectic day. I was in the middle of managing a large conference. I stared at the screen. Really?! Some judge in a little city in a strange country is going on vacation, so we need to completely start from scratch? What would this do to my business appointments and commitments? And those hard-earned flights? We'd have to start all over again now.

What I wanted to do was call it quits. How dare they make this change! It just wasn't right. Or fair. Do they know or care that we have a life? Who could I call to complain?

Fact was, there was no one to call. No one cared about my schedule or my flights. Or my feelings. We hadn't even left yet, and already I was at my breaking point.

So this was the way it was gonna be, huh? One obstacle after another, and it didn't matter at all how I felt about it. I could sit there and complain, but it wasn't going to make any difference. So, my choice was to either keep fighting a fruitless battle, or try to find some new way of dealing with this. I was entering territory where logic and fairness weren't the point. The only point was adopting the kids. I had to start adjusting...to trusting.

So, right there, in the client's tech room, I remember putting my head down. I took a breath and, rather than fighting it, I complained to God instead. I realized I could not "project manage" this journey like my job. I resolved to calm down and take it one step at a time. After a minute, I really did feel better. It was time to start all over.

And so we did. I got home and jumped on the phone again with US Air. It took several hours of conversation. It was pretty stressful because now flights using miles on those specific dates might not be available. Without the miles, it would mean thousands of dollars in additional cost.

The client control room where I had my epiphany.

The good ladies on the phone worked hard, searching all possible flights to help me secure seats. So much clicking of keyboards! It was touch and go for a long time. Option after option fell by the wayside. Finally, new flights...using miles. And the awesome part about it? Because it was last minute, there were no coach seats available, so we were upgraded to business class. That's right, business class, baby!

It was such a wonderful surprise. It felt like a gift, like a little reward from God because I was trying to have more faith.

I resolved to complain to God more often.

6. Here We Go!

Monday, August 2, 2004
Posted by Mike

Can you believe this? Two mild-mannered Mainers, traveling halfway around the world to bring two children home. Who knows how this will go? We'll do our best to keep you posted on all that transpires.

Here is our itinerary for the first week:

- Wednesday, 8/4: Boston to Frankfurt, Germany
- Thursday, 8/5: In Frankfurt
- Friday, 8/6: Travel and arrive in Almaty, Kazakhstan
- Saturday & Sunday, 8/7-8: In Almaty
- Monday, 8/9: Meet officials in Almaty; night train to Taraz
- Tuesday, 8/10: Arrive in Taraz and see kids for the first time

There will be more content coming...assuming I can get online over there. My best guess is you will see a lot of blog content starting on the 10th. Hopefully, I'll be able to get a good connection.

So, the next time you hear from us, we'll be venturing into the unknown.

How are we feeling?

Nervous. Worried. Wondering if we completed all the documents. Thinking about our three kids we're leaving here in the US. A little excited to be traveling someplace new. Oh, and a *little* apprehensive about the fact that our lives are about to change forever.

— NOW —

Why a blog, anyway?

I, Mike, have journaled since I was 11. I was intrigued about
writing a "public" journal. I also think it was necessary for my
sanity to write about the experience. It was my way of imposing
some kind of order on a situation where there was very little.

*MIKE: I like technology, and this gave me an excuse to buy a new
laptop and a camera. It was a lot harder to blog back then! I really
didn't know if I could even get online in Kaz. And forget Wi-Fi. You
needed a phone line and a modem inside your computer. The speeds
were slow. Uploading one picture took minutes, not seconds. I had no
idea how blogging would work. But I was certainly eager to find out.*

HEIDI: This moment was years in the making. For so long I
wondered, would now be the time to adopt? The answer was always
not yet, not now. Births and miscarriages marked the first years of
our marriage. Our first pregnancy ended in a miscarriage. Two more
miscarriages happened between the birth of our first two children,
Zack and Jake. After our third child, Brynn, we experienced two
more. We knew, after the last one, that we were ready to be done
with that part of our lives. When the time did come to adopt, we
would request children younger than Zack, Jake and Brynn so it
wouldn't upset the natural birth order. Why create more issues
unnecessarily? We were getting closer.

Next, we focused on building a house big enough for five children.
It's not just parents who need to be approved in the home study.
Your home needs approval, as well. Building our house took longer
than expected (not surprising, right?). Once it was finished we were
now ready to start the adoption process. The moment where it all
came together had finally arrived!

*MIKE: The first miscarriage ended our very first pregnancy. That early
loss was painful and it permanently changed our outlook on all of life.
Most young couples simply expect to get pregnant and give birth. We
didn't know if we would be able to have any children at all. We now
knew, there were no guarantees. Our life would be different, and we
decided to own it. We were so thankful for Zack, Jake and Brynn.
After the fifth miscarriage, we both knew it was time to end, and to
begin.*

7. And So it Begins

Wednesday, August 4, 2004
Posted by Mike

We left home at 2:00 pm and got off the bus in Boston at 5:45 pm. We had to get our tickets reprinted due to our change of plans and, thankfully, that went without problems. We're scheduled to leave on time at 9:40 pm. Right now, we're sitting in an airport lounge, waiting to get the call to start boarding and, since I can get online, I thought I'd write a quick post.

Before we left, we took a picture of our four little bags and our three little children. We worked hard to pack everything into just four bags to make sure we would have no checked luggage. It's always best to have everything you need with you, if possible. Forgive me if I am a little prideful in our packing prowess.

So, we're traveling light. But man, I'd give anything to be carrying those three kids as well.

We are sitting in the lounge waiting to go to the gate to board. I look around at the people, the food, and listen to the English language. This is the last time we'll be in America for quite a while. We are heading to a place with different people, different food and a different language. A bit too much to take in! Time for another hot dog before we go.

HEIDI: Excitement, uncertainty and sadness were all around as we said our last goodbyes. Four weeks was a long time. The push and pull, wanting to stay and wanting to go.

We are fortunate to have a wonderful extended family. At that time my sister and brother-in-law, Amy and Peter, lived a stone's throw away and they watched Zack, Jake and Brynn. My mother and father, Barbara and Roland, also helped take care of them.

MIKE: I was trying to play it cool in the post. In reality, I was really having second thoughts. Were we being irresponsible parents, risking our lives by doing this? What if something happened to us? I was feeling pretty guilty leaving those little ones. Once I got on the plane, I made a mental decision to put those thoughts out of my mind or I'd be a basket case. The choice was made. It was time to go forward.

Fearing for my kids. It would be a recurring battle throughout the trip. It was a good thing I didn't know how hard it would be without them. Because it was really hard.

HEIDI: We also packed "essentials" for ourselves like a mini plastic Bodum French press, coffee and PowerBars. And toilet paper. We had no idea what we'd be able to buy. What more does one really need than coffee and PowerBars and TP, anyway?

Giving a small token of your appreciation has long been a custom in this part of the world. We require that you bring six, **$20 plus or minus gifts for women and ten additional small "token" gifts, maybe $10 each,** again mainly for women as well. 95% of the people you will deal with will be women, with the constant exception being your driver and an occasional judge, so having 1-2 non-gender specific gifts is advisable.

Information on gift giving from our agency.

Much of our luggage was filled with gifts. We packed presents for baby home staff, for our two children, and for all the kids in their groups. It was difficult figuring out what was appropriate. In the end, I chose products Maine is known for, such as pine sachets, and items with maple syrup and pictures of moose and lobster. For the children, I brought blow up balls, stickers and many more kid friendly items. For our two children I brought cool toy figures called Bendos.

Practice Packing?!
Mike "practice packs" before every trip. No checked bags = no lost bags. To this day, our kids will show us their tiny bags when they go on the road. We did something right!

8.   Hot Dog! We're in Frankfurt!

Thursday, August 5, 2004
Posted by Mike

What? You groan at my pun title? I make no apologies. On three hours sleep, THAT IS HUMOR. I wear your mockery as a badge of honor, *Herr American.*

Yes, we are in Germany for the night. We arrived around noon, and had a fantastic time schlepping around this surprising city.

Before today, Frankfurt, or "Bankfurt" as it's been called, held little interest for me, other than a layover on the way somewhere else. But we had a great time today touristing. There's a lot more here than I expected. Even though the temperature was in the high 80s, it was very refreshing to be back in Europe again. I love this continent.

Tomorrow morning the trip begins in earnest. We leave for Almaty at 11:50 am. We land at 11:45 pm, Kaz time. Using frequent flyer miles limits flight options, so we are arriving early. As a result, we'll have the whole weekend to ourselves. While we'd rather be home with Zack, Jake and Brynn, we plan to make the most of our extra time and see this new part of the world.

I have to admit, I'm beginning to look forward to heading east. I've never been further than Hungary, so this is indeed stretching our boundaries. We have a driver all weekend who is meeting us at the airport. We hope he shares the English language with us, but we really don't know. We want to see the city of Almaty and, if all goes well, some of those mountains that look so enticing in photographs.

Heidi is winding down in the hotel room as I post this. We're staying at a Marriott and, because I'm a platinum member, we got a great upgrade. It includes the executive lounge access, which we're taking full advantage of. Our dinner tonight consisted of a lot of free hors d'oeuvres, canapés, snacks, and, in the interest of better cultural relations, some German beer. So, membership does have its privileges.

I wonder what our accommodations will look like in Kaz? Probably not as nice as our suite here in Frankfurt. So, I'll enjoy it as long as I can. *Gute Nacht!*

HEIDI: Mike and I both love to travel. For several years, I met Mike in a European country after he'd completed one of his business projects. Although comfortable with travel, we knew this trip would be like no other. I cannot think of anything that would have prepared us for just how different and challenging this travel experience would be.

MIKE: Being in Western Europe was an awesome way to start the transition away from home and into a new culture. I really enjoyed our day in Frankfurt, but I carried this tension with me the whole time, knowing what was coming. It was like some low, foreboding music playing in my head all day.

As we walked around, we tried to be the same casual tourists we were used to being. But that wasn't possible anymore. We weren't there to appreciate the culture. Instead, we were just killing time while we waited to get on a plane and jet into a different life. And we felt that pressure, even though we couldn't explain it.

I finished posting and crawled into that Marriott king-size bed, having no idea what to expect the next day. I didn't sleep very well. I might have been worried. Although it could've been the beer and schnitzel.

Our top ten favorite European cities
We love Europe! Here's where we suggest you start:

1. Venice. Our first trip. Go off-season (dang tourists!).
2. London. We love everything. Except the high prices.
3. Barcelona. The light, architecture, La Sagrada Familia.
4. Paris. It really is romantic. Write at an outside cafe´.
5. Grindelwald. A beautiful Swiss village. Great skiing.
6. Rome. Chaotic and wonderful.
7. Budapest. Take a night river cruise; magic.
8. Ljubljana. A charming storybook setting in Slovenia.
9. Košice. A hidden gem in Slovakia.
10. London. We love it so much, it's on here twice!

9. When Five Minutes Feels Like a Lifetime

Saturday, August 7, 2004
Posted by Mike

We landed in Kazakhstan at 11:00 pm. The flight from Frankfurt was easy; two movies and you're there. As much as we wanted to go to sleep, we forced ourselves to stay awake to adjust to this new time zone. It worked...kind of. In any case, *Starsky & Hutch* made me laugh out loud. When you're in a metal tube 30,000 feet up, humor comes cheaply.

The Almaty airport is a very nice, new airport. I was expecting something from the Khrushchev era, so it was a welcome surprise.

The customs guy studied my visa for a loooong time. So you try to be cool and casual while you wait, but not TOO cool, not cocky-American-flippant. Finally, he passed us through. We had only carry-on luggage, so we breezed right out to arrivals. We entered a sea of people.

So. When does five minutes feel like a lifetime?

When it's five minutes looking for your driver, that's when. I've had drivers in many countries, and sometimes they were late. But, when it's midnight in Kazakhstan, and swarthy taxi drivers are eyeing you as a potential large fare, AND you really have no idea where you're going even if you decided to take them up on their offers...well, you get a little hot under the collar.

I calmly (at least I hoped I appeared that way) strolled around the crowd, looking for a sign with my name on it. It seemed all I saw were names spelled like "AZΣAΩ3ΘZA." As the minutes ticked by, I began to think worst-case scenario. I spied a driver from the Hyatt Hotel. I knew that was the only Western hotel brand in the city (or country!), so I determined to NOT let that guy leave without us. If I couldn't find my driver, we'd be leaving with him.

So, I'm keeping one eye on Hyatt boy, and one eye out for my name, while strolling casually through the Almaty airport at midnight. Yes, five minutes went by verrry slowly.

At last, I saw a young guy in the back of the pack, talking with a girl, holding a white sheet of paper in his hand. The paper was blank, but—wait! Was there a "V" on the back side??

I walked up, gesturing for him to turn the paper around and—yes!! Yes!! It said VAYDA! We are NOT going to a Kazakh prison! We are NOT spending the night on the streets of Almaty!

I didn't hug him—at least, not hard.

Vitali (our driver's name) explained that he "was not seeing us" because usually adopting parents a.) have lots of luggage and b.) are dressed in t-shirts and flip flops. God knows how long we would have been waiting if I didn't spy that "V" on the back of the paper.

From there, it was an easy trip to the apartment. We got to bed around 2 am, trying to grasp the fact of where we were.

I dreamt of swarthy taxi drivers.

> luggage bypassing customs completely. If you are carrying over $6000 then there is a small customs area to the right of baggage claim where you will go and present your form and baggage. An officer may ask you a few questions about what you are doing in Kazakhstan, what is in your luggage, etc. They may not ask you anything and simply waive you on. As I said, do not fill out a form unless you are carrying over $6k - it is not

Our agency instructions made it sound so easy!

HEIDI: What we could not say in the post was how nerve-wracking it was getting through customs (we talked about that experience at the beginning of the book). Why were we carrying so much money, you might wonder? Well, there are many fees and costs in adoption. What we were carrying was the fee for the Kazakhstan agency.

MIKE: Looking at the cost, you may be thinking, "Hmmm. Did things really need to cost that much? If so, why?" The cost of adoption is an uncomfortable topic. It can sound like someone is "buying" children. That's not true, at all. Foreign adoption is a very complex project. And when you are in a foreign land, you are at the mercy of how things are done in that country. It's a humbling position, to say the least. I did wonder how those funds were distributed. But I will say that, while we were in Almaty, everything seemed legitimate and professional.

> **You must try your best to get NEW bills for this trip** The money exchangers are *very* particular so make sure you talk with your bank about getting new $100's or $50's or as new as possible, $20's are acceptable as well, of course you will carry a great deal more. Some exchangers will even give you a lower exchange rate because your money is older.

Those "NEW bills" were burning a hole in our money belts.

HEIDI: We were required to hand-carry that amount all the way from home. This means we had ten thousand dollars, EACH! Doing the math, that's twenty thousand dollars! Our agency wrote us and said, "You must try your best to get NEW bills for this trip. Money exchangers are very particular... Sometimes the teller will reject a perfectly good bill because it has a mark on it." They also stressed that the cash "must be presented in brand-new, unmarked bills." Obtaining cash in this form was a real challenge! At first, our local bank gave us a hard time trying to get the "new, unmarked bills." I was in tears at times trying to get what we needed.

Finally, it was suggested (I can't remember by whom) that I contact the Federal Reserve Treasury Department in Boston. I spoke with a woman who was so kind and understanding. Miraculously, that did the trick. When we went back to our bank they were suddenly able to help us, and our request for new, unmarked bills was promptly granted.

MIKE: *There were several times like this during the adoption when we were at the end of our rope and something good happened that was completely out of our control. I tried to think of a catchy name, but it's really simple: Grace. Undeserved and unexpected, but so sorely needed. It happened when we got business class tickets. And it happened here, as well. We don't even remember who suggested we call this Boston federal agency. All we know is that we were able to get that cold hard cash. And we were grateful.*

HEIDI: The next problem was, how were we going to carry these new, unmarked bills all the way there? Mike and I are big fans of Rick Steves, who writes travel books. He always recommended wearing a money belt. We would joke about that whenever we traveled. Who in the world would wear a dorky money belt? Um...that would be us!

We love Rick

For our first trip to Europe in 1998, we bought a ton of books;
the one we used was Rick Steves. Practical, concise, and witty.
Now, whenever we travel to Europe, the first (and only book) we
buy is Rick's. We could've used him in Kaz!

MIKE: *Those money belts aren't as easy to put on as you think. We can report that there is a right way to wear your money belt...and many wrong ways. We developed our own strategy of negotiating the straps and clips and zippers. We wore them all the way to Almaty. That belt was a constant companion under our shirts. Like people pat themselves to make sure they have their phones today, we were constantly patting our tummies for the reassuring feel of the belt.*

HEIDI: If anything happened to that money...? As we kept telling ourselves and each other, there's no point focusing on "what ifs." All we can do is be extra vigilant and alert. We would deal with what happens when and if it did. The scariest time of all was in the customs office of the Almaty airport.

It was one of those experiences that felt like it would last forever. Our minds were begging, please, please give us back the money! And, in their sweet time, they did. Phew!

> After you answer their questions you will be free to proceed to the exit where your driver will be waiting for you. You will be able to see them from the baggage area, which is separated from their waiting area by a glass wall. They will be waiting with a sign with your last name on it.

Just like they told us...piece of cake!

As hard as it was for two planners like us, up until then we had resigned ourselves to following the process. The agency controlled everything. They did a great job of telling us the exact steps to take, and when to take them. That worked, right up until we stepped out of customs, into a sea of people speaking a language we did not know. It dawned on us...we have no idea WHO would meet us and we have no idea WHERE we were going! We did our best to squelch the rising panic.

MIKE: *What sticks with me was how alone I felt in that airport. I remember looking in Heidi's eyes, knowing she felt the same way. We had no one to call. We needed to rely on each other completely. We had been married for about 15 years, but we had just entered a whole new realm of trust in our relationship. It truly was just the two of us. We had to lean on each other.*

Here are some quotes from our agency documents:

> "**VERY IMPORTANT!** While in Kazakhstan DON'T DISCUSS your adoption in any manner...DO NOT leave your paperwork laying around...please remember this...there are many groups and government agencies working feverishly to STOP international adoptions from Kazakhstan...We know that you would never willingly do anything to jeopardize adoptions...all it would take would be a minor slip up to someone in the news media. The rules are simple, don't discuss your adoption with anyone but our main people..."

All of this is running through our jet-lagged minds as we try to NOT look like American adoptive parents!

It was a great relief when we sank into the backseat of our driver's (Vitali's) little car. It was even better when we sank into the bed in our apartment.

I lay there, trying to wrap my head around where we were. A new land. Kazakhstan! And, why we were there. We were going to adopt two little people and bring them home. What else would we face on the way? Too much to process for my travel-addled brain, for sure. I fell asleep.

10. How Do You Spell Relief?

Saturday, August 7, 2004
Posted by Mike & Heidi

I've been to enough new and strange places to know that things are always intimidating until I get out and see the area. Walking around is kind of like marking the territory for me. So, we decided we'd get up around 7:30 am to do just that before we got picked up for our first meeting. We awoke at 9:45. So much for marking the territory!

Heidi is here to talk about the apartment (pictured above): *When we arrived, it felt a little scary outside because we arrived at the back of the building. The three flights of stairs were dark and bare cement. We basically collapsed into bed. We woke up to bright sunshine. The apartment is clean, modern, and feels safe (pictured above). It looks out on a main street, and it was nice to see normal daily life going on, even in a very foreign country.*

Mike here again. Our driver, Vitali then took us to the meeting.

We met with Galbanu, one of "the Sisters" here. The Sisters are NOT nuns, as we first thought. Rather, they are three lawyers who act as the official contacts/organizers/managers once you are in-country. She was very professional, very kind, and very nice to meet with us on a Saturday. We began the paperwork, which will conclude on Monday. After that, we had the whole day free.

HEIDI: At the office, the very first thing we did was take off our money belts and hand over the cash. I can't express the utter relief it was to have that money out of our hands and into the hands of the right people!

It is funny what the mind conjures up about foreign places. I had imagined a tiny out-of-the way room with a person sitting behind some nondescript desk but, instead, we witnessed a fully functioning office with several workers intent on their tasks. This Almaty-based agency seemed to operate quite like any in the United States. In retrospect, it makes sense as it takes a load of people, talent and space to get the job of adoption done.

MIKE: *Speaking of what the mind conjures up, boy, did I have the wrong picture of "the Sisters!" Whenever our Geogia agency referred to the Almaty office, it was always about "the Sisters." We both pictured them as nuns, but my mind took it a little further. I created a mental picture of a castle, three nuns in habits, solemnly singing chants and lighting incense. Imagine my surprise when we walked into a modern office and an attractive, well-dressed woman rises to shake my hand! Heidi and I laughed a lot about that afterwards.*

I had mixed feelings about taking off my friend Mister Money Belt. He had been with me through so much! Not to mention, it's not too easy to hand over all that money, either.

HEIDI: Okay, since we've been talking cash, this is probably a good time to address the elephant in the room. How much money does it take to adopt?

In 2004, our adoption totaled (drumroll, please)...forty thousand dollars! AND another ten thousand expected in travel expenses. Yup, fifty thousand dollars. You can understand why using frequent flyer miles was so important! Those miles saved us a lot.

MIKE: *That's a big amount of money to come up with! Fortunately, we had planned ahead. That, of course, was the key. My business was going very well. And the US adoption tax credit of $10,000 per child at that time was a big help when April 15th rolled around.*

I had a strange conversation about adoption costs before we left. We were at a picnic when a relative (who shall remain nameless), asked, "So Mike, how much do two kids cost?" No one had put adoption in those blunt (and tasteless) terms before to me. I looked at him and said, "About the same as that new sports car you want to buy."

How we spend our money tells us what we value. What we add to our lives defines our lives.

I knew Heidi had wanted this all her life. We felt that, if we had the financial means, why the heck wouldn't we spend our money trying to save two kids from a horrible future? Becoming an adoptive parent pulls you out of so many worlds you thought you would always stay in (like being a white family). Some worlds are hard to leave. Others, like being ignorant about adoption, I was happy to leave behind. So, the contents of Mr. Money Belt was an investment in the kind of life I wanted to live.

The Good Life: Clarify

__Clarify__ is the third Element to living the Good Life.
It means to craft a simplified life where everything fits.
A few years earlier, I was spending money in the usual
"American" way: improving my own life. This adoption journey
changed my priorities about money and possessions for good. I
live more simply, and it makes me feel more free.

HEIDI: Meanwhile, back at the office, we were glad to get going on the final paperwork. Now is a good time to talk about the dossier (pronounced, "dos-ee-ay"). I had not heard of a dossier until we started this adoption process. It is a packet containing all the necessary documents required by the adopting country. There were about twenty separate documents that made up our dossier!

Nearly every document required a notary and an apostille. All documents had an expiration date. I was constantly checking the dates of each one. If any of them was even close to expiring, it would need to be renewed.

The dossier had to be in a specific order and it MUST be in that precise order! If not, the entire dossier would be returned. If that happened, we might wait longer and that in turn could jeopardize the timing of the adoption and possibly the adoption itself. Many a night I woke in a sweaty panic fearing a document had expired!

__MIKE:__ Endless paperwork! Heidi handled the bulk of it, and thank God she did. I've always hated red tape, and it seems to me adoption is the mother of all bureaucratic jungles. Every day Heidi was sitting at the dining room table with dozens of papers strewn about her. I did my part by staying out of the way as much as possible.

"Apostille": A new swear word

Getting something apostilled is basically another way of proving
it's really you signing the papers, like an additional notarizing.
Why isn't notarizing enough? Who knows? We never even heard
of an apostille before, and suddenly it's ruling our lives. Over
and over, we filled out paperwork, got it notarized, then drove to
the state capital to get it apostilled. To this day, "apostille" is a
dirty word in our house. It's right up there with the F-bomb.

HEIDI: And then we'd get a call saying they needed "one more thing."
So, we did the process all over again. FedEx overnight again. Over
and over and over. Would the paperwork never end?

The FedEx guy, our new best friend!

MIKE: *Apostillin' paperwork...*

11. Western Decadence & Horse, of Course

August 7, 2004
Posted by Mike

Our driver Vitali is a nice guy and a Godsend. Imagine, for a very small sum, you have access to a car and an English-speaking driver who will take you wherever you want to go! And even better, since you have NO IDEA where you want to go—he'll suggest places!

Our first stop was a very "Western" mall. By that I mean, American. The amount of decadence and avarice was right up there with the best (worst?) of our malls. (But, I had to admit, it was kind of nice to see Pringles.)

Vitali thought we would like to eat at the food court in the mall (I guess most Americans do?). What?! Come halfway around the world and eat pizza?! No, sir. We wanted a real, authentic Kaz lunch. He seemed puzzled, but shrugged and said okay. It took him awhile to decide, but he took us to an incredible restaurant.

The atmosphere was really cool; they prepared the food in an open kitchen. The smells alone were intoxicating. We tried five or six different things, each wonderful. The food was really, really good. All kinds of strange and tasty things. Some of it reminded us of Chinese food, other times of Middle Eastern, other times of Polish or Ukrainian. It was all good. All good.

Now, I feel a little bad about upstaging the rest of the meal for some grandstanding. But if you can't come to Kazakhstan, eat horse, and then boast about it, well, what's the point? Yes, the final dish contained horse meat. We didn't ask ahead of time, and Vitali didn't

44

say anything. I had a hunch this wasn't beef or lamb, like we'd already had. But I ate it, anyway.

It was only afterwards that I asked him, "Okay, my friend. Tell me. Did we eat horse?"

He smiled and said, "Just a little."

How was it, you ask? Not nearly as weird or freaky as I imagined. No, not like chicken, either! It was kinda like a tougher beef. Not great. Not bad.

Now, will I make any childish jokes about it?

Neigh, I say! Neigh!

From there, we drove around Almaty, then headed back to the apartment. Heidi and I walked around awhile longer, found a store, bought some ice cream and some cream for our coffee. The only reason I know it's a cow-based product is because there's a picture of a cow on the bottle. I figure, hey, it may not be cream, but it's from a cow. Call it good.

The other big adventure today was the hour or so we spent trying to figure out how to call home. As a recovering techie (okay, okay, I'll always be a techie), it bugs me TO NO END when I cannot figure technology out. Even the cell phone I brought wasn't dialing through! And the message in Russian wasn't helping.

As I fumed and railed against the country's phone system, Heidi called a second number (that I dismissed as "not important"). Turns out, they spoke English, and my bride learned of the need to add a mysterious "8" during the dialing sequence. That did the trick.

As we wind down, we plan to watch an hour of our 24 DVD, and (hopefully) get a good night's sleep.

HEIDI: The show *24* with Kiefer Sutherland as Jack Bauer was a thrill-a-minute TV series that took place in real time. Twenty four hours in *24* shows.

MIKE: Our laptop had a DVD player and my sister suggested it was a good show. So I bought Season 1. This was before streaming was a thing. (The internet speed was so slow while we were there that it wouldn't have mattered anyway.)

HEIDI: It proved to be a necessary distraction. Our one escape we could always count on. And, as you'll see, we definitely counted on it!

As far as Almaty was concerned, Mike and I found the city exhilarating. With the exception of phone issues, we enjoyed every minute of our first day.

MIKE: In my mind, there's nothing as exciting as travel. Here we were in the most foreign country we'd ever been in, and loving it. All day long, I kept thinking, "Mike man, you're in <u>Kazakhstan</u>!" After dropping off the money, I felt like I had been set free. And being jet-lagged made the whole day a hazy, happy joy ride for me.

Top Kazakhstan First Impressions
1. The signs with their weird letters (and numbers)
2. The people. Very few Caucasians!
3. A lot of light blue-colored buildings
4. Left-over Soviet atmosphere and architecture
5. And, of course, the horse.

12. The Hills are Alive...
with the Sound of Vaydas

Sunday, August 8, 2004
Posted by Mike

There are times when traveling that you take a step back, kind of outside yourself, and think, "This is cool. This is an adventure, and I really appreciate the opportunity to experience it."

That happened today.

It didn't begin until noon, however. I didn't roll out of bed until 9:45 (again!). I was really feeling the jet lag. That, and the fact we didn't get to bed until 11 pm. We shouldn't have done it (and now it's too late to stop), but we managed to pull ourselves away after the first two hours of the first season of 24. This show? It's dangerous. It's that good. We find ourselves talking about it the next day ("You know, I'm thinking that father with Jack's wife is up to no good!"). I can tell right now, this is gonna be a great diversion over the next few weeks.

Two cups of coffee really helped and, by the time Vitali came at noon, we were both ready to go.

Yesterday was a bit cloudy, but nice and cool. Today dawned clear, which was perfect, because we were heading to the mountains. We couldn't see them in the distance yesterday due to cloud cover. We began to drive outside the city, and the clouds returned. As we drove up the hill (very steep), the clouds really obscured all but the closest scenery. Still, it was beautiful. We continued to drive up to a ski resort. When we arrived, we happened to meet another American couple here adopting, with a different agency, which was a big surprise. The four of us then took a ski lift for a better view.

It was still cloudy at the end of the first lift, so the other couple stayed behind. Heidi and I took lift #2 and, halfway up, the clouds parted, revealing a stunning view of massive mountains. That was enough for us to decide to take the third and final lift to the top of the mountain.

Remember what I wrote at the start of this post? Well, halfway up the third lift, both of us were just blown away by what we were seeing. And that's when I was smart enough to realize what a gift it is to be able to experience this. I say, without a doubt, it was on par with the beauty of both the Bavarian and the Swiss Alps. Way cool.

We decided to hike back down to the second lift, then met up with the other couple, and had lunch at the base of the mountain.

Again, fantastic food. The Russian soup (no, of course I can't remember the name!) was great.

Upon returning to town (a short 20-minute drive), we finally found the café we were looking for last night, and we had excellent cappuccini.

One final funny thing before I finish. As we reached for the outside door of the apartment building, we noticed with surprise that it was closed...and had a combination lock on it!

We looked at each other. In my mind, I recalled seeing something about a "key code" on the welcome sheet. Which was safely upstairs, in the apartment. Nobody said it would be needed here! In fact, we never saw that door closed. (Hello! There's a DOOR here!)

Heidi remembered something about a "2." I recalled there being three numbers. So, we began pushing the buttons. Of course nothing happened. We were stuck.

How long would we be out there? How would we explain what happened to a local without knowing Russian? And who would we explain it to? The contact number for Vitali was, of course, on the welcome sheet. Safely upstairs. In the apartment.

I began looking around the door frame, and found three numbers written. Cool. Try those three. Nope. Try a different order. No. Try them backwards. *Nyet.* Now what?

I thought maybe there was a "reset" to start over, so I pushed a few of the buttons together.

Heidi said, "Maybe you need to push all three at once."

"Nah," I said. "Who could do that with a bag of groceries in their hands?"

As she is often wont to do, she ignored me and tried anyway (like the phone adventure of yesterday, for instance).

Et voila.

Lock is opened.

We thought that was pretty funny. And, yes, even though we were laughing, both of us were saying the same thing in our minds, "Thank God."

Otherwise, we might still be out there.

So tonight is our last night here in Almaty until the eve of our return.

I have to say I am impressed with this city. It's no NYC, of course, (what else is?) but it certainly is cosmopolitan, multicultural, clean, safe, with a surprising amount of culture, restaurants and beauty.

I hope to spend a few more hours outside tomorrow before we go. But I will leave here feeling a little less cocky in my Western-ness. And a little more humbled. The world is bigger than I thought. And there's so little we in America see. Or really want to see. To think that halfway around the world there is a rockin' city like Almaty that I never knew or even heard about until a year ago.

The world doesn't revolve around us.

Go figure. ;)

HEIDI: This is a good example of what makes travel, adventure.

New places bring new perspectives. We were taken out of ourselves and our everyday lives allowing an alternate view of the world. Travel comes with risk, though. Risk of not knowing whether a particular experience will be "good" new, or "not good" new. Our day involved both—wondrous mountains and locked doors. Almaty was an unexpected pleasure.

MIKE: Just a great travel experience. To this day, I remember that feeling of breaking through the clouds into sunlight as we headed up the mountain.

Being there just felt...exotic. These were mountains I had never seen before! I honestly kept thinking that I was the first American to be this far away, to be seeing these beautiful things. I knew it wasn't true, of course, but I couldn't shake the feeling. Here I was in this new land, seeing new sights I never dreamed I would get the opportunity to see. I felt special, privileged. Travel is such a wonderful thing.

What a gift, before we had to get on the train to our new life.

Almost Olympic

Did you know that the two finalists for the 2022 Olympics were Kazakhstan and China? It's a shame Kaz didn't get picked. I could have boasted of being on an Olympic ski mountain for decades to come.

HEIDI: Even though we were having such a great time in Almaty, Taraz was ever present in the back of our minds. We knew why we were here, and it was coming very quickly.

MIKE: This was the fun part. Yes, we were in a new country. But now, the real journey to the new life was about to begin.

13. "The Change is Gonna Do Me Good..."

Monday, August 9, 2004
Posted by Mike

As Heidi and I sit on a 1950s-style Soviet-era train, waiting to leave for Taraz, I've been thinking of the post title. It's a line from an old Elton John song (and I am kind of a Honky Cat, aren't I?). Or maybe it's better to think of the Sheryl Crow song (*"Change'll do you good"*). Or...maybe Little River Band? (*"Time for a cool change"*).

Sing with me! Whatever song you choose, we're in for a big change soon.

Taraz, where the two children are. Where *our* two children are.

Just a quick ten-hour (haha) ride on this train, and then, sometime around 9 pm your time Monday night, we'll be meeting the two children we are adopting for the first time.

How does one prepare oneself for this? I'm all ears. ;)

Right about now, I think you go into a sort of autopilot mode. You just, like the Heat Miser from the Christmas show, put one foot in front of the other.

And soon we'll be walking in the door. Of the *baby house*.

Can you feel the tension? :) We'll keep you posted!

HEIDI: The train was outdated, much like we expected. The facilities are always a question in developing countries. Would there be a toilet or simply a hole in the floor to squat over? (Turns out, it was a toilet.) We also didn't know if it was safe to leave our belongings unattended, since our facilitator walked us to our berth...and promptly disappeared. Fortunately, our evening was uneventful and she did reappear to wake us in the early morning.

"The Spanish Train"
We kept hearing we would be taking "The Spanish Train." It sounded so romantic! But, we also heard about the train conditions Heidi mentioned. In the end, we never did find out why it was called something so enticing, and yet be so...not.

MIKE: *Three memories from that train ride.*

First, watching our facilitator, Galina, leave and tell us to lock our door, and realizing, we had no idea how to find her! It was a panicky feeling. What if we needed...something? Anything? We felt very alone.

Second, we mentioned that Taraz was on the Silk Road, a crossroads of East and West. The Spanish Train was taking us to Taraz, to a crossroads where we had the choice to begin a different life, to change the direction of things forever.

Third, I woke up in the middle of the night and watched the terrain flow by in the ghostly moonlight. We didn't know anyone; we couldn't communicate with anyone; we were going to meet our new children in this strange land. Somehow, though, watching the plains scroll by to the clicking of the wheels, I felt...at peace. Life should be an adventure, I thought, as I drifted off to the gentle swaying of the Spanish Train.

Questions to consider
"Off you go then" is about Mike & Heidi changing direction to get closer to their Good Life. What are some examples of this? Where are you going "off to" in your life, and would you change it if you could? (For more questions and your **free** *study guide, go to* **NotFar.org/Kaz**)

Part 2

At the crossroads

14. "Show Me the Children!"

Tuesday, August 10, 2004
Posted by Mike

Our ten-hour train ride was actually pretty nice, if you have the right expectations. We took a couple Excedrin PM and slept most of the way.

At 3:30 am, our facilitator banged on our door. We packed, stumbled out the door, through the hallway, and onto the platform as the train slowed to a stop. We were whisked to an idling older-model Mercedes as the rest of the train was just stirring. It definitely felt like something out of a spy movie. When the car stalled, I felt like I should panic and yell, "go Go GO!"

However, the car quickly re-started, and we were taken to our hotel. I don't think we were followed. (Or *were* we...?) We slept for a couple hours, then dragged ourselves out of bed, enjoyed a refreshingly brisk shower, and then were driven to the baby house.

Okay. I hear you: "Enough! Blah, blah!! Tell me about the kids!!!"

It happened Tuesday morning, 10:00 am our time.

We were brought into an office. Three or four women were there. After ten tense minutes, many nails gnawed, and 97 anxious glances at the empty doorway, the children...yes, our children...were brought in.

I had my video camera sitting beside me and I pressed "record."

Two very nervous, very wary little children appeared at the door. They were being pushed a bit. Not strong-armed, per se, but clearly they would have rather done this whole thing more slowly (if at all).

I wanted to speak for all four of us and say, "Geez, give us some room! Give us some time to ease into this thing!" I didn't say that out loud, of course. In any case, these tiny three-year-old children were thrust upon us amidst lots of women speaking Kazakh to them.

I could only make out two words, but at least they were very important ones: "Momma. Poppa."

Thank God our expectations were low. I hope other adoptive parents don't expect warm hugs and kisses with a breathless, "Father? Mother? Oh, thank God you came! Now; when shall we leave?"

It's clear that the kids were as whacked about this whole thing as the parents were—probably more. We were told they were expecting us, that they understood what it meant and, by this age, all of the children here eagerly awaited their day of adoption. Still, it HAD to be overwhelming.

Our first impression? Both of us were thinking, how small they are! Even though we knew they were underdeveloped, they still looked awfully tiny.

At least they didn't burst into tears at our first meeting, so we could consider it a success.

The tears? Well, they would come soon enough.

HEIDI: We had no idea what to expect. With little sleep, little information, and a lot of anticipation, we waited. Mike and I sat together on a saggy sofa. Other people, possibly workers, were standing around the room. Then, there they were. Two children, just looking at us in the doorway. Time stood still as they inched their way to stand directly before us.

I felt sorry for these two terrified beings! My heart wanted to gather them into a big hug but my gut said they were scared enough. They were so tiny for three year olds! I kept wondering, "What are they thinking?" They looked so anxious. I wanted to ease their fear by giving them space, yet they were "encouraged" to hug and embrace us. This moment felt awkward and uncomfortable for all of us.

Greeting these little ones for the first time was also awkward because of their names. Mike and I had chosen new first names. Their Kazakh first names would become their middle names. For weeks leading up to this moment, we had referred to them as Nik (Nikolas) and Meg. Greeting them as Sergazy ("Sieer ga za") and Zhansaya ("Djun sigh yah") felt weird and actually difficult. Mike and I called them by their given names while there, though, and it did get easier.

MIKE: *Surreal. I know it's an overused word, but this was like nothing I had ever experienced before. The office was quite cold and sterile. We were already dazed and confused from the train ride and lack of sleep. No one spoke English, so we had no guidance or instruction. We simply sat and stared at the empty doorway, waiting for our new life to appear in the form of two little children. Talk about waiting at a crossroads!*

"I love adoption!"

It really did seem to take forever for them to appear in that doorway. We'd hear voices...a worker would walk in, then back out. Many times. Each time, we'd expect to see the kids...and then, they wouldn't show. It was maddening. I felt like Tom Cruise in *Jerry Maguire* (hence the post title). I wanted to scream, "Show me the children! I love adoption!" Although, I don't think that would have helped.

We heard voices of women and the shuffle of little feet long before we saw them. The noises echoed down the hallway. I don't know if the tension could be cut with a knife...but it was certainly something I felt. Shuffling. Voices. Empty doorway. More shuffling. Voices. Doorway. Repeat.

When they did appear, they had to be pushed.

What I remember most is tiny little Nik putting his hand up to his forehead as he stood there. Almost like, "Oh Lord, this is really hard!"

They were nudged all the way to us as we sat stiffly, waiting. Meg at one point actually seemed to push back a little with her shoulder. Ah, a rebel! Then, they were right in front of us. Little eyes looking anywhere but at the people in front of them. All four of us just kind of froze. What do we do now?

I wish I had been more...loving? Approachable? Kind? Welcoming? Instead, I just felt like a lug. I simply did not know what to do! They were lifted onto our laps. I showed Nik the camera screen, and he seemed intrigued. Or maybe it was a welcome distraction from the tension. The voices of the women cooed and soothed. The only words we understood were "Momma" and "Poppa." We tried to make the moment less awkward, but I assure you, it didn't help.

In a few minutes, they were lifted off our laps, and we all stood up to go...somewhere. We didn't know where, and no one could tell us.

And that was our storybook introduction to our new son and daughter!

I don't know how the first introductions go for other adoptive parents. If this was a crossroads for the four of us, it was closer to a train wreck than a smooth merge. But, we all survived the meeting, and no one backed out.

I guess it could have been worse.

And, it was. Read on!

15. Day One, Part Deux: Olympics & Apples

Tuesday, August 10, 2004
Posted by Mike

(This post continues the first day.) After a few minutes, the children were led out ahead of us and we followed. We were directed into a sort of music/play room.

Soon, Nik's entire "group" was led in—about 12 children in all. Meg sat next to me, as she was still in the younger group (she's four months younger than Nik).

We were then treated to a play. It was very, very cute. They sang, they acted out parts, they did a little mini-Olympics—quite entertaining.

A guy was videotaping and I hoped it might be for us. Occasionally, he would put the camera on us, so we did the frozen-smile thing. I felt like Dan Quayle during that vice-presidential debate with Lloyd Bentsen.

The most memorable moment happened when I reached out to hold Meg's hand. You could tell she was pretty nervous about this. She warily side-eyed her hand in mine. But she didn't pull away. After a few minutes though, she let go to do something. Ah, a perfect excuse to stop without offending the new Poppa, I thought. But then, to our surprise, she put her hand back in mine. If there

59

was a moment when I got a little misty, that was it. I know a brave act of faith when I see one.

After the program was over, all the kids left—except for our two. As the last caregiver left, she motioned to us, and we interpreted it to mean something like, "Bonding Time veel begeen NOW!"

The door closed.

Everything went swimmingly. For all of two minutes. The videographer was still there, so this is all on tape somewhere.

Every child had been given an apple during the play, and now our two children were gnawing on theirs like it was a race for their lives. It was a tense time, and they were getting through it by putting all of their attention and mind power into eating...the...apples. Who would win?!

Sounds of chewing filled the air.

Both lil' Kazakhs were gnawing to beat the band. This was well and good—until Meg, who was winning the race, suddenly starts choking. Just a little bit. Juuusst enough to make you think, "Is she...?" Then, it becomes obvious.

She's got too much in her mouth and she's not getting it all down! Now, what do you do as a new parent? Well, communicating is out, since you don't speak their language. If you run out the door for help, are you disqualified as a parent? What to do?

And, all the while, the cameraman is still rolling.

It starts to get a little scary, because obviously she's having problems, and not feeling too confident that WE are going to be of any help at all. Just at the moment when I am ready to call 911 (or whatever it is in Taraz), with Heidi's help she seems to recover and hacks up a large ball of squishy apple mush into Heidi's hand.

Well!

After that, the kids clearly knew we were useless. Meg begins to cry very loudly, her little legs shaking from her near-death experience. She slowly makes a casual move towards the door. Will we stop her? Well, should we? We don't know. We're new here.

When she senses the weakness, she pounces. She moves quickly to the door, still crying, and then, poof, she's gone.

Nik, who has been nervously gnawing on the apple, now realizes he is alone. As the camera rolls, he stays brave for one long minute. Then, he whimpers, looks vacantly at the carpet, and slowly makes his move to freedom. In a flash, he is gone, too.

Only the apples remain.

And Camera Guy. After an embarrassingly-long minute of the clicking sound of the tape wheels turning, Camera Guy mercifully presses stop and leaves too.

Thus ended our First Official Bonding Time with Nik and Meg.

Just like in those heartwarming adoption movies, we have started our new Forever Family!

— NOW —

HEIDI: The little play they performed came as a relief. For a few minutes we were not the center of attention (except for the cameraman). I thought, how nice that we'll get a video of this life-changing event! And it certainly would have been, had we ever received it. That recording of our first hour with Nik and Meg would have been a true treasure for our family. What was its purpose? Was it to see if Mike and I were bonding with Nik and Meg? Was it some kind of official visual documentation? Was it for propaganda purposes, for how successful adoption was? If so, they certainly wouldn't be using this footage! All these years later and we still don't know. I guess we never will. One more mystery.

The tension and discomfort were palpable when the four of us (five including the camera guy) were left alone in the room. All the while I was paying attention to the amount of apple Meg had in her mouth. Wow, that's a lot of apple! And sure enough, she began choking. Did she often choke? I had no clue what was normal for her and what I was supposed to do to stop it. I bent her forward and began patting her back with some force and was utterly relieved when the mushy apple and saliva mixture landed in my hand.

Within minutes of meeting our two children Mike and I already felt like failures. With no way to communicate, a choking episode and their subsequent departure did not seem like a good start at all!

Speaking of apples...
This is a wonderful book by Christopher Robbins. We highly recommend it. It tells a lot of interesting, funny stories about this country and its people from a Westerner's perspective. And about apples.

MIKE: One reason we're writing this book is so people will know what adoption is really like. It's glamorized in movies. You see scenes of "Forever Families," and "Gotcha Day," and the first meetings are simply perfect. Sure, adoption is an amazing thing. But sometimes it ain't pretty. This first experience with our kids was quite disheartening. I could have been really discouraged after that. Instead, I kept thinking about how funny this was going to sound in the blog. That thought—"This will be a great story!"—helped me stay detached from how horribly wrong this was going.

A few terms

"Forever Family" refers to orphans being adopted and becoming part of a family, for good! "Gotcha Day" refers to the day of adoption, when the parents "get" the child. These are phrases that can sometimes gloss over or downplay the challenges and difficulties of adoption. They can also set up unrealistic expectations. In our case, at least, we found the phrases more ironic than sincere. But that's just us.

HEIDI: Some situations are funny only in hindsight. I chuckle when I recall Nik and Meg edging for the door. I imagine them thinking, if I walk slowly enough, these two people won't notice. It cracks me up...now!

16. Baby Steps... Baby Steps...

Tuesday, August 10, 2004
Posted by Mike

When I last wrote, we were leaving from our first visit feeling not only very tired, but trying hard not to be discouraged. To be honest, even though our children ran out of the room screaming, we really DID believe it would get better. It couldn't get much worse, could it?

We got back to the hotel and absolutely crashed. We slept right up until it was time to head back to the baby house. We were not feeling our chipper best, but we splashed some water on our faces and headed out.

We were led to that same music/play room, and I hope the caregiver didn't hear us both sigh at the same time! We sat down and waited for them to bring the kids back in.

Nik came in first, and I immediately brought out a toy: a little bendy-guy. Thankfully, he made a beeline for it and instantly it became the most fascinating thing he had ever seen. Hey, he's not crying? Mission accomplished.

They brought Meg in, and, you guessed it, she immediately started to wail. It seemed Heidi and I had the same exact thought. It was like, okay, enough. We've been parents for almost twelve years already. We can handle this. As I began to say, "Heidi, go over and hold her," Heidi was already going. It was the right thing to do.

64

Did she stop crying?

Heck no.

But it made all the difference in establishing exactly who was the momma, and who was going to be in control.

And people say there is no God?! Come on! At least ONE of you had to be praying at just that time, cause, believe you me, it was a piece of divine inspiration to do that on Heidi's part. It made the afternoon bearable.

For the rest of the afternoon visit, we walked outside, we played inside, we sat, we stood. And, Meg pretty much cried no matter what we did.

What-ever.

While outside, they were given another apple. NO! We almost screamed. But, lo and behold, there was no choking this time.

In the scope of our adventure thus far, this was a huge victory.

The best news? They stayed with us the whole allotted time. Not one escape attempt!

As Bill Murray repeated over and over to himself in the movie, *What About Bob*, "Baby steps ...baby steps."

After the visit, we changed hotels. Doing so will save us about $700 over the course of the trip, and this new room seems to be fine. It has the one necessity I must have. It has A/C.

And now, safely tucked into our little hotel room, with the air conditioner whirring soothingly in the background, watching 24 is going to feel so, so good.

HEIDI: When Meg began crying, I decided to do what a mother does. Pick her up and hold her, regardless of the response. I figured, she cannot cry forever! Eventually she would warm up to us, right?

This had to be a distressing time for Nik and Meg. Being with two strangers who call themselves Momma and Poppa. How weird for them. And what does it even mean to have a momma and poppa, anyway? They certainly didn't know.

I forgot that Mike titled this post, "Baby Steps." I can't tell you how many times Nik and Meg have watched *What About Bob*?! They absolutely love this movie! Nik and Meg mimic the scene of Bill Murray eating corn with the family, when he utters over and over, "MMMM, MMMM, MMMM!" If you have not yet seen What About Bob, then it is time to take "baby steps" to enjoy the movie yourself.

Our agency assigned us the "best" hotel in Taraz since Americans tend to have higher expectations. For us, it was too formal with its high ceiling and tiled floor. We inquired about other options and were shown The Zhambyl Hotel. Their room was cozier with A/C, and a window overlooking the city. And less expensive, too. We'll take it!

Home away from home
It was a great decision to change hotels. We have fond memories of our stay at The Zhambyl. It was a sanctuary for us. Because of the advice to keep a low profile, we kept to ourselves almost exclusively.
(We wish we didn't.)

As is not uncommon for me, I moved some furniture around to make the space more useful and comfortable. However, each day housekeeping would do their thing and we'd return to find the furniture back in its original location. Moving furniture, like opening curtains, became my new daily ritual. It gave me a bit of control and that made me feel better.

MIKE: *That first day was exhausting. It was such a whirlwind, from the overnight train, to the spy-movie Mercedes ride, to a few short hours of sleep, to seeing our new children, to almost losing one of our* *new children to a choking death, to another nap, back to the baby home...it's like we were being pushed around by the experience repeatedly. That's why it was a real turning point for Heidi to step in with Meg. It was the first time in that long day that we didn't feel at the complete mercy of outside forces. Maybe we wouldn't be horrible parents to these kids, after all? This was another grace thing. We needed some wisdom, and somehow got it. It was our first steps down our new life path.*

The Good Life: Power

Power *is the seventh Element to living the Good Life.*
It means to plug into a system to live the Good Life daily.
We needed a system in Kazakhstan, but it would be a never-ending dance during our time there; the country would push us back on our heels, leaving us bewildered. Then we'd shake our heads to clear the cobwebs, take a breath, and find some small way to take a little power back. On second thought, it wasn't a dance. It was more like a boxing match!

17. Class, it's Time for Review

Tuesday, August 10, 2004
Posted by Mike

So.

Maybe you're thinking, "Good. They got the kids. Must be time to pack up and head back to the good old US of A, right?"

"Great story, Mike. Cute kids. Congrats. See you in a few days...?"

As they say in Taraz, "Au contraire, mon frère." (Or something like that.)

This is Kazakhstan, baby. You have to really, really bond with these children. You have to show you are truly committed to them.

So, how long do you think that requires? A week?

Yeah, that's what I figured. You know, seven days, two visits each day, two hours each. That should do it.

No.

Two weeks? More than enough time to bond with the children...and the caregivers...and the cook...and everyone in town. Right?

Try three weeks. We are here for three more weeks.

If all goes well, we will go to court on August 31. If approved, the children will be officially "Vaydas."

Okay, you say. So THEN are you coming home?

Uh, we are. The kids aren't.

You see, there needs to be an official "waiting period" of 15 days that goes into effect after court.

Why? Um, because. Just because.

You can either stay the additional 15 days, or you can go home and come back.

I think you will understand when I say most parents come home, if only because they have foolish things like, oh, say, jobs. Children. You know, a life. But, I digress.

Then, after the fifteen day waiting period, Heidi will come back, this time with her mother, to get the kids.

Then do they come home?

Sure.

Right after finalizing the paperwork back in Almaty.

All told? She'll be gone another 11 days.

So, in a nutshell, if all goes well, with no surprises or delays, we will ALL be back home by late September.

Or before the snow flies.

My wife is telling me to be wise, and leave additional comments unsaid at this juncture. Wouldn't be prudent. And I will do just that.

HEIDI: I hoped to adopt from a country that would let us see firsthand where our children lived. Because our required visits were actually in the baby home, we were able to do that. There are countries where parents meet their children for the first time somewhere other than the orphanage. It might be in the hotel where the parents are staying or in another prearranged place. My first thought is, why doesn't that country want you to see their orphanages? The answer to that question worried me. The less you know, the less history you have about your child.

It is more than unfortunate that, in those situations, the adopted child will be the one to bear the brunt of so little information. Fortunately, not only did Mike and I see the baby home, we spent time with our children there. The place that was their "home" for the first three years of their life.

The Good Life: Be

We got to personally see the conditions and routines and watch our children interact with other children and caregivers. I am grateful to Kazakhstan for this. Mike and I were able to share what we saw of the baby home, country, and culture with Nik and Meg while they were growing up.

When we first started the adoption process, the visitation requirement was two weeks. That changed to three weeks, and then the fifteen-day waiting period was also added. These requirements did seem excessive. It felt like a lack of consideration for parents who needed to make a living in order to adopt. For us, the extended requirements meant we were away from Zack, Jake, and Brynn even longer.

It was explained that the fifte-day waiting period provided the opportunity to reconsider the adoption. It's hard to imagine a scenario where prospective adoptive parents, after going through one to two years of paperwork, meetings, home study, the cost, and three weeks of visiting their child would then change their minds. This fifteen-day waiting period added more days, more expense, and more travel. There were parents who chose to stay for the duration. That could be less expensive but, if there were any glitches in the process, those parents were essentially stuck. Situations like this caused some parents to have awfully long stays.

MIKE: *As I mentioned before, my relationship with authority has never been a good one. My first question when faced with a rule is never "Yes, Sir!" It's "Why?"*

This process was very onerous on adoptive parents, as Heidi explained. And when I wrote the blog post, I was feeling quite ticked off at the rules.

To be honest, I can see some American privilege in my words, and I'm not proud. I'll own that. Still...who makes up these rules anyway? Who decides that this amount of time is the right amount for a good adoption? Who are the men (they are usually men, aren't they?) who gather in a smoke-filled room (the room is always smoke-filled, at least in my mind) and decide, "Yes! It makes perfect sense for adoptive parents to spend months here!" The cynic in me hears store registers ringing. The longer we're in-country, the more cash money stays, too.

Do I think it was necessary for us to be there that long? No. Do I think it made any difference in our decision-making process whether to go through with the adoption? Of course not. We had already made the commitment hundreds of apostilled documents ago (sorry for the inappropriate language, using the "A" word). I will say, though, that going to the country, and experiencing it, was such a benefit. I am very glad we did.

Just, not for so dang long.

I'd say ten days would've been about right.

The sad thing was, I'm already complaining in the blog at the very start! It certainly would get a great deal harder. Clearly, the adoption honeymoon was over...and it wasn't a very long honeymoon to begin with.

To use the journey metaphor, we really wanted to get moving into our new life! Instead, the four of us would be sitting at the crossroads in Taraz together for weeks to come.

Know before you go!

Oddly, I, Mike, didn't really pay close attention to the details before we left. Maybe it was just overwhelming. If you travel to a new place, it's well worth scrutinizing your plans ahead of time. Knowing helps you set realistic expectations. That reduces complaining, and makes the trip more fun.

18. We Luuuv Surprises!

Wednesday, August 11, 2004
Posted by Mike

So, for the next *twenty days*, our schedule will look like this:

- Sometime before 10 am: Crawl out of bed.
- 10:30 – 12:30: Bonding time
- 12:30 – 3:15: Lunch, free time (in other words, "nap")
- 3:30 – 5:30: Bonding time
- Evening: Escape into the world of 24.

The evenings will eventually include more than just 24. But these first few nights, believe you me, Jack Bauer has been our best friend.

We were warned that the Kazakh people like to surprise you. They like to spring things on you at the last moment. Why? Maybe they are a spontaneous culture. Maybe it harkens back to their nomadic roots.

Maybe they just like to tick you off.

Who knows? In any case, they definitely seem to operate under a "need to know" basis. And obviously, we need to know at the very—last—minute.

Take, oh, this morning, for instance. We get in the car for our morning visit and Galina, our facilitator, tells us we have a meeting with...the Baby House Director.

Now, we were just told the day before that there would be no meeting with the director.

What-ever.

How do I describe the director? As you can see in the picture, she is quite—regal. She wears her hair in the Taraz-ian style, a B-52s, 1960s-style bouffant (really; even the younger girls wear it like that at times). She has an authoritarian air about her. I guess if I said her name could be "Imelda," would that help?

We were assured this was a friendly chat, but it sure didn't feel that way. After a couple of very direct questions, I realized I needed to treat this like a formal business interview. It lasted about ten minutes, and we walked out saying, "Ta heck was that all about?"

We learned a phrase recently, and we say it a lot: Be a leaf in a stream. Do NOT fight the current. Leaf in a gosh dang stream...

The visits went better today, though. Heidi immediately went to Meg and picked her up, and spent most of the time holding her.

Nik is a quiet boy, and seems quite industrious. So far, he seems much more easygoing. But he can get upset in a quiet way. He's a real sweet child.

Our interpreter, Ildos, came and will be with us for the afternoon visits with the children. Good thing. I forgot to mention that we were told the kids (and all of Kazakhstan) speak Russian. No, Galina says. They only speak Kazakh. Well, we don't have any dictionaries for Kazakh.

This will be even tougher than we thought.

We stopped at a toy store (so to speak) and bought some blocks, as we are realizing that two-hour sessions go awfully slow if you don't have more toys.

The evening? Need we say what we watched?

— NOW —

HEIDI: Mike and I were so tired after our morning "bonding time" that we'd return to the hotel, eat a PowerBar, and take a nap before our afternoon session. Two visits a day and unexpected, impromptu meetings took all the energy we could muster. This might sound terrible but time with the kids really dragged! It was hard to keep them entertained with so little verbal interaction and little to do. Purchasing toys did make it easier.

When we attended the required weekend workshop back in Maine, the recommendation was to "be a leaf in a stream." Mike and I repeated this phrase again and again. Sometimes humorously but, more often, facetiously. We didn't know what to expect from one minute to the next. I think most adopting parents have got to be planners/preparers. I don't know how one could get through an international adoption otherwise. There's such disparity between intense planning and preparation to absolute last-minute, spur of the moment meetings and events. Surprises that would take an emotional and physical toll on us.

Although our international agency had worked in Kazakhstan for some time, Taraz was a newly-opened region for them. I believe we were the first couple from our agency to adopt from Taraz. Mike and I were the guinea pigs and it felt like it!

For months leading up to this trip, Mike and I attempted to learn a little Russian. We brought our Russian/English guide only to find that Kazakh was the predominant language spoken in this region and by our children! Now we were completely reliant on the translator to communicate with Nik and Meg. Every day I wrote down words and phrases I would need to interact with them. Bathroom, hungry, toys...the list grew longer and longer as I envisioned myself on a plane with two children and, one day in the not-so-distant future, at home with no one to translate. Yikes!

MIKE: Have you ever seen "The Truman Show"? The main character realizes he is in a world full of actors, and they are all conspiring to keep him hostage. That's how it was starting to feel. We were beginning to understand that no one, literally no one, was for *us. What I mean is, there was no authority figure to go to for help, to get clarity, even to get a simple explanation! I know we had a "facilitator," but we rarely saw her and, when we did, we'd get cryptic partial answers to our questions. It's like she was making it up as she went along. (Come to think of it, maybe she was. We were the first parents going to Taraz, after all.)*

The Good Life: Own

The first few days were a chilling realization that we were absolutely on our own in this movie, and it was feeling like there was no director in charge to make sense of it. In fact, we just met the director, and she wasn't what we needed. For two planners like us? A sickening feeling. We realized, it was up to us to look out for each other.

The director of the baby house was a real trip. First of all, seeing her wearing the hairdo of my mother from 1968 was a culture shock.

I compared her to "Imelda" in the post, knowing that people back home would think of Imelda Marcos. She had been the wife of the president of the Philippines. They really did look a lot alike (you can look her up).

A great band!

For those of you not growing up in the 70s, my reference to "The B52s" was about an awesome band from that time period, and the two women wore their hair in a similar style. For fun, go listen to *Love Shack* or *Rock Lobster.*

The director clearly had power. You could sense it. We, of course, had no idea if we could "trust" her or anyone else. So our answers to her strangely-probing questions were very guarded. Oh, and she had a gold tooth, as well (I'm not making this up). So it was easy for my over-active imagination to think of her as an ex-Soviet KGB agent or something. I'm sure she wasn't. Probably. And she was likely a very nice woman.

At home.

19. We <u>Do</u> Love Surprises. We Do...

Thursday, August 12, 2004
Posted by Mike

Surprise!

As we got in the car this morning, we were informed that it was time to take the kids to get passport pictures taken.

Like, immediately.

The kids haven't been in a car, maybe, ever. And now we are to take them into the city for pictures?

The good news is that, though they wailed like they were dying at first, they didn't push away from us. We weren't the enemy, it seemed. It was actually funny how much both of them cried and cried; the pictures weren't the best quality as a result. I hope immigration officials at the airport don't judge the kids' willingness to be with us based on the passport photos!

The cutest thing of the day was to see how suddenly Nik burst into a smile when he was told the picture-taking was done. He's got a very winning smile. (And I do hope to show you. I am uploading one picture at a time, so please be patient. It may be awhile.)

This evening was a real treat. We learned that there is an American family in Taraz who lives here permanently. They have a non-profit that provides business assistance to Taraz as it moves further away from the old Communist ways toward free enterprise. We had dinner at their house and it was so refreshing to talk with fellow Americans.

We learned a number of very enlightening things about Taraz and Kazakhs in general. This couple has been living here, with their four children, for eleven years. When I told them about our "guidelines" while here, they smiled. They assured us that Americans are very welcome here, that we have nothing to fear. They could tell we were not the stereotypical loud rude Americans, and they encouraged us to get out and about to see the city (good news, except that it has gotten very hot today; maybe when it cools down).

They also told us that every person in Taraz speaks and understands Russian. True, there is a move toward more Kazakh language, but, yes, we could probably speak a few Russian words and be understood. (Which was exactly the opposite of what we heard the day before!)

We had a great time, and we hope to visit with them again.

It was even worth missing 24.

HEIDI: Mike aptly described our excursion to get passport pictures of two very frightened children. This trip meant something else for Mike and me. It meant we would NOT be in the music room. Yay! Getting passport pictures made us more hopeful that forward progress was indeed being made.

How refreshing it was to be with a down-to-earth American family, in Taraz! It was kind of them to welcome us like that. One of their boys reminded us of Jake, our second son. A piece of home!

Locals: A gift from above
Meeting this family was the greatest "grace gift" of all. We can't imagine surviving the trip without them. When you travel, do your best to find a "local" guide or contact.

Enlightened is right. What we heard about Taraz from our new American friends was a refreshingly different perspective. We had been told to be careful! Do not go out after dark! Stay close to the hotel! What was so threatening out there? Especially since, day after day, I people-watched from our hotel window and I wasn't seeing anything all that threatening.

My hunch was that fewer potential issues would arise for the agency if adoptive parents remained low key and out of sight. Instilling fear in adoptive parents is a good way to accomplish this. I guess.

MIKE: *Boy, did we need that visit with the American family! Just when I was feeling so isolated and on the verge of paranoia, here comes people like us! We weren't in "The Truman Show," after all. When we got back to the hotel, I felt a small glimmer of hope.*

Traveling to a foreign country can play tricks on your mind. When you have no one to talk to about your concerns, or give you a bigger perspective, your fears can define the experience. I guess that's why it's called "culture shock." I'll say it again: thank God for that family.

The Good Life: Plot
Plot is the third Element to living the Good Life.
It means to map out a plan to create your unique Good Life.
This excursion was the first time I felt like the kids weren't
uncomfortable with us. Nothing like a mutual crisis to bring
strangers together!

20. Everybody Has an Opinion

Friday, August 13, 2004
Posted by Mike

This morning's visit, we planned on spending as much time as possible outside. The weather has suddenly become surprisingly cool, especially in the mornings. So we headed outside with our new toy blocks. We sat under a tree on a bench, and the kids sat down on the sidewalk and dug into the blocks.

As we sat there, one of the caregivers came by. She stopped and began talking (in Kazakh, of course, not Russian) and gesticulating wildly. We didn't need to know the language to get the gist: the children MUST NOT sit on the ground! They MUST sit on cardboard or on the seat!

Oookay, tiger.

We were warned that children are considered public property in this country, and people do not hesitate to give their opinion. We bit our tongues, smiled, and had the kids sit on their haunches, instead.

Eventually, this could get annoying. But we realize this will be a bit of a tug of war as we all adjust to the changing authority and changing relationships. The caregivers are wonderful, and you can tell they really love the children. I'm sure they're already cutting us a lot of slack, at least from their perspectives.

Galina stopped by briefly. She informed us that she would be leaving us to go back to Almaty in two days. So, we'll be in a hotel where no one (and we mean no one) speaks English. We were again cautioned to keep a very low profile; to not go out after dark; to be very careful what we do and where we go.

It'll be interesting to know how we are to fend for ourselves within this straightjacket—I mean—within these guidelines.

HEIDI: And just when you think you know what's going on...wham! It feels like what they're really saying is, "You clearly don't know what you're doing. Everyone knows children never sit on the ground! And you think you're qualified to be parents?" Insecurity floods the mind.

Fighting these thoughts took effort! Rationally we knew and understood the cultural differences. We were already parents but that knowledge didn't help much when incidents like this happened. I can't imagine how difficult it must be for first-time parents.

Ah. So *that's* why...

Kazakh culture says that sitting directly on the ground is indecent because the ground is considered filthy...and is believed to cause sterility. Clearly, coming from the US, that conclusion would have never entered our minds!

MIKE: So this is how it would go while we were there: you'd be really discouraged because of surprises and changes of plans; then, you'd get a little burst of hope (like the American family), and then you'd get hit with a whole new set of surprises and strangeness. And we're back on our heels once again. Back on our heels, but NOT, of course, back on the concrete. God forbid.

HEIDI: And our facilitator is leaving?! Are you kidding me! Why would she leave us with no contact person? This was unsettling and maddening! Seriously, you expect us to stay in our hotel room all weekend? It is a good thing we connected with our American friends or we would have been completely freaking out!

MIKE: You can probably sense from the post that we were frustrated. I knew I wasn't supposed to be so honest online, but we were really having a hard time. There was not one single person in that hotel we could communicate with.

A lonely feeling, indeed.

21. Montezuma Vacations in Taraz

Saturday, August 14, 2004
Posted by Mike

I hate to say it, but Montezuma's Revenge isn't limited to Mexico. Yes, I'm struggling a bit, in that, uh, area. I even stayed in the hotel this afternoon instead of going for the visit. As I write, I'm hoping things will, um, work themselves out.

Our facilitator leaves today. We will officially be on our own.

This morning, we learned that Meg announced to her entire group that she now has a Momma and Poppa and they don't. We're not sure if we should be touched by her announcement or disturbed by her attitude. We'll find out, I'm sure.

We have a set of photos of our family, our house, etc. that we will show the judge when it's time for the hearing. We have been taking the pictures to show the kids each visit. Heidi tells me that, this afternoon, they were very animated as they looked at them. She said Meg was pointing to my picture and saying, "Poppa." Nik loves looking at the "machina," our minivan. Get used to it, Nik buddy. You'll be spending a lot of time in there with four other kids!

Heidi also said they were trying to say the kids' names. They seem to be able to say, "Zack" and Nik was even saying "Jake." "Brynn" may take a little more time.

Tomorrow is Sunday. We only have one visit scheduled. Yes, we actually get an afternoon off! We hope to get out and walk around for the first time.

One last note: We have a meeting with the Department of Education on Monday. We are assured it is "informal and casual."

And I have a bridge in Brooklyn at a very good price for you.

HEIDI: Our facilitator was leaving, Mike was sick and now I had to entertain two children in the baby home, alone. Ugh. I mean, it was hard enough when two of us were there!

Why not cancel? We were informed that, if we missed visits, we would have to make them up. ANY days added on would most definitely result in missing our already scheduled flights back home. This, as you can imagine, was the last thing we wanted!

MIKE: "Montezuma's Revenge," for our younger readers, is a euphemism for intense diarrhea. Being physically sick in a foreign country, especially in a country as foreign-feeling as Kaz, was terrible. Like most men, I am a total wimp when it comes to illness. But it really was bad; I literally could not leave the bathroom. I was weak and I had zero energy. Thank God Heidi was there. I can't even imagine how it would have been if she wasn't.

The problem with local food

Watch enough Netflix food specials, and you'll believe that street food is perfectly safe everywhere! That's simply not true. I, Mike, don't know where I got the illness, but it almost certainly came from eating local food. The best advice: when in doubt, avoid anything to do with unbottled water (even salads and brushing teeth). And just like in the US, if the food joint looks sketchy...don't go there.

HEIDI: It was touching as Nik and Meg began to put names and words to the pictures I showed them. These pictures represented a new life coming soon for Nik and Meg. I wasn't sure how much they were grasping, but it was a step in the right direction.

What were Mike and I to make of Meg's declaration that she had a momma and poppa and the other children did not? This was another instance where we realized we knew so little about these two kids. They were strangers to us just as we were strangers to them. Only time would change that.

MIKE: I have a confession to make. Being so sick was almost worth it, because I didn't have to sit in that blasted music room that afternoon. Almost worth it, if I didn't spend the entire time sitting on, or laying by, the porcelain throne.

HEIDI: We were determined that, come hell or high water (or Montezuma's Revenge), no visits would be missed!

22. Is it Really a Sunday?

Sunday, August 15, 2004
Posted by Heidi

This Sunday is certainly not the usual Sunday. With the morning routine down—shower, coffee, time to journal and pray—off we go again to the baby house. Montezuma's visit continues for Mike, though he does make it to the baby home with me.

We go to the rooms of Meg and Nik and find they are outside. We go in search of them. We have Meg go to "Poppa" and she bursts into tears. Now, why's that? Who knows! We go outside for a walk and play on a slide. Neither one seems too into it. We have them sit to play and Meg begins to cry. I pick her up...uh huh...now I know why she cries...*twa-let!* We go inside and her caregiver changes her and we all go back to "the room." I hold Meg and her crying dissipates. Maybe she intuits her "Momma" had a crying spell earlier this morning herself and wanted to join in.

We called Zack, Jake, and Brynn last night, which was great. It brings to mind though how much we have missed them and are still missing them today.

"Time for lunch," the caregivers say (in Kazakh), and off Meg and Nik go. "See you tomorrow guys," we say (actually, we say "sowbool," which is "goodbye" in Kazakh).

Because Mike is not feeling so swell, we opt to stay in our room instead of seeing the sights of Taraz this afternoon. We have two more Sundays here and hope to sightsee then. So instead, for fun, we ordered the Kaz version of chicken soup (not bad, either!) and green tea from our hotel and took it easy.

We just returned from a short walk around town and bought a few items at a nearby market. Mike is beginning to feel a bit better, at least for the moment, which is good news.

I sit here writing this while looking out our hotel window. The Hotel Zhambyl (pronounced "jam-bull") sits on one of the main roads in Taraz and overlooks a big park, a bar, a couple four-story apartment buildings, and two yurts (tent-like homes). People go in and out of these a lot, but I don't know what the yurts are used for here in the city. I watch the people, what they are wearing, how they walk, and it keeps little by little seeping in where I am. In some ways it is unbelievable to be sitting here seeing what I see and yet...I am. Wow!

Mike is off his deathbed and making a few comments:

About that "informal" meeting tomorrow afternoon? You guessed it. It seems a bit more formal, now that we know the questions that may be asked. I am trying not to think of this as a trial! Also, we have been requested to dress up more than usual. What, no flip flops? :)

This has been a bit of a tough day, but we are hanging in there. I mean, how bad can things be when you have another episode of 24 to look forward to?

We hope that all of you have a relaxing, peaceful Sunday. Please, enjoy the afternoon with your family. Hug your kids. Buy them an ice cream and tell them they're cool. You'll be glad you did.

And that you are able to.

HEIDI: This particular Sunday was a low point that involved some tears on my part. Out of our normal schedule, our minds were freed up to consider home. How could we leave our three children like this? Were we crazy? What were we doing? We missed Zack, Jake, and Brynn so much. We missed our weekend routine. And we dreaded (maybe that's too strong a word, but it's close) another week of what felt like snail's-pace progress, interrupted by periodic anxiety-producing meetings.

It was a difficult and disappointing weekend. All week we looked forward to sightseeing that Sunday afternoon, but Mike's illness changed that. Visiting Nik and Meg on my own Saturday, followed by a less-than-satisfying Sunday morning visit, was dispiriting. Sightseeing was out. Being near the bathroom was definitely in.

About those Yurts...

Visible from our hotel room, they were places to purchase a local favorite, fermented horse milk. It's believed to have medicinal and digestive qualities. We wish we'd tried it. Who knows, maybe it would've helped Mike!

We were excited when we connected with Zack, Jake, and Brynn. It wasn't what we talked about as much as just hearing their voices. I was filled with reservation and doubt after we said goodbye, though. We were so far away. Worry, homesickness, and missing our kids crowded my mind and pervaded the day.

MIKE: That was a tough day, for sure! As tedious as the visits to the music room could be, at least they provided routine. We suddenly had all this time on our hands, with nothing to do.

I think it gave us a chance, for the first time, to begin to process all that we had been living through since we arrived. Up until that day, we had simply been reacting to what was right in front of us. That Sunday gave us the chance for reflection. Like Heidi sitting at that window and crying, the reflection was a hard one to look at, for both of us. We ached for the comfort of a simple, quiet Sunday at home with our little ones.

23. Ups and Downs

Monday, August 16, 2004
Posted by Mike

This morning's visit with the kids was a much better one. We stayed outside, which helps. (The music room gets very stuffy. Stifling, I say! Of course, Heidi says I'm overreacting.)

After Meg rejected me yesterday (no, I'm not hurt at all), Heidi says we need to be more aggressive in our bonding with the kids. We're the parents here, and we should be setting the example, not the kids. So today, we spent more time holding the kids and giving them hugs. It DID seem to go better. No outbursts of tears this time, and we had a good visit.

Now, any rational adult would know to expect ups and downs in this bonding process. Not me, however. I expected a steady upward curve of bond-ation. So, as is the norm in this process, I need to adjust. Adjust.

If I'm any more adjustable, by the end of this trip I'll be that Bendo toy that Nik likes so much.

We have our "informal meeting" this afternoon. We'll let you know how much fun we all had when we return.

Maybe we'll all play badminton? Tag?

MIKE: *Let me be honest. I really dreaded going to that music room (as if it wasn't obvious already). It was an empty room, with only the toys we brought with us for the kids to play with. Any sort of "bonding" would happen because we were all prisoners together in that stifling room. The minutes dragged by. So it was a great idea to get outside, and it made us all feel better.*

HEIDI: One visit would go well, then the next was filled with crying and discontent. I think emotionally all four of us had our ups and downs during these visits.

MIKE: *It was an odd act we were all playing. Here we were, two Americans who spoke none of the language, walking slow laps around the baby home, smiling wanly at anyone who walked by. What did they think of us, I often wondered. Were we welcome there? Did they resent us? We never found out. The workers were never anything but kind to us and to the children in their care.*

Unless, of course, we deserved a scolding, and those were included at no extra charge.

The Good Life: Be

HEIDI: About Meg rejecting Mike; sometimes we reject what we need the most. Children need mommas and poppas. How awful that Meg didn't have them! Now, she was turning her back on the person she desperately needed, her Poppa! This Momma and Poppa were committed to a posture of acceptance even if they might turn away from us, and even if it felt like rejection. Mike and I hoped that, with love and time, issues of abandonment, rejection, and fear could be overcome.

24. A Very "Informal" Meeting

Monday, August 16, 2004
Posted by Mike

So, on the way to the meeting, our interpreter (pictured above) tells us, "I am very nervous." He says that there will probably be seven or eight people questioning us.

Crap. If he's nervous, what should WE be?

We enter a big building on the city square. We sit down and he tells us, "Be quiet and try not to draw attention to yourselves."

I had the strangest urge to stand up and belt out *God Bless America*. I don't know why.

We wait for over 25 minutes. Finally, a woman comes downstairs and yells at us to rush upstairs. The desire to walk slooowwwly comes over me, but I fight it off and walk briskly up the stairs. It seems like a lot of other people are following us up the stairs, but I could be imagining it.

We enter a room, and there are only three people seated there (later, we learn that three of them were sick. Good for us! Montezuma...?). The chairperson, a woman, motions for us to sit. We do. Our interpreter tells us to stand. We do. We sweat. A lot.

The questions they ask are things like:

What do you do for a living?

How many children do you already have?

(You should have heard the murmurs when we said, "Three." Amazing! So many!)

Why do you want to adopt?

Why two, instead of one?

Are you aware that they are not well?

Are your children happy about the adoption?

Do you want to keep the Kazakh culture alive for your children? How?

The questioning went on for about ten minutes. We had been warned that they COULD HAVE, but did not ask, "Are you adopting the children to sell them?" Uh, no.

They seemed fairly friendly, and they finally said they saw no reason not to recommend us for adoption, and that they would recommend for the judge to proceed. They wished us luck, and that the children would meet our wishes for happiness.

We said, "Spasiba," which is "thank you" in Russian, and walked out the door. As soon as the door was open, I was faced with several dozen people who had indeed followed us up the stairs. They apparently were all trying to get in to see the same people we were!

As we headed out, I don't know who was more relieved. Actually, I do. It was our interpreter. The look of relief on his face was almost comical. Why?

The chairperson? She was his mother.

MIKE: *The interpreter is nervous because our interrogator (interviewer, whatever) is his mother! You can't make this stuff up. At times like this, I felt as if I was in a Monty Python skit. It started as absurd, and it could go in any direction at any moment.*

The ordering around was very hard to take. Wait here. Sit down. Don't smile. I found myself thinking like a teenager. I wanted to rebel. It was the lack of communication and the lack of control that were the hardest things to deal with. That afternoon, sweating in my suit, was an experience of both. And it was hard.

Having said that, it was one more necessary, but bizarre, meeting that was now finished.

HEIDI: We had expected them to ask, "Are you aware these children are not well?" One of the many documents we signed was an acknowledgement of the medical and social risks of adoption. Tests and medical diagnoses in foreign countries can be unreliable. Possible diseases and conditions might include milk intolerance, under-stimulation, malnutrition, mental illness, retardation and HIV. There were over *thirty* potential conditions on the list. Remember when we spoke with the doctor from Boston who told us all the problems foreign children could have? From Kazakhstan's standpoint these children are "sick." The extent, severity, or degree of that "sickness," though, is unknown. This would be left for parents to find out.

MIKE: *I saw that document as a way for our agency to basically say, "You're on your own. Whatever you get, we're not responsible." I don't blame them. They made it clear that Kazakhstan was willing to release only their "sick" children for adoption. We were warned that, anytime we were asked that question, our answer needed to be, "Yes."*

But it wasn't clear how true that was. Here's the conundrum: were the children allowed to be adopted because they were sick, or were they diagnosed as sick in order to be adopted? Was it necessary to justify to powers-that-be? We never learned.

HEIDI: How they defined "sick" was not only broad, it was unclear. Here are a few of the diagnoses on Nik and Meg's birth information we received:

- Respiratory insufficiency
- Perinatal encephalopathy of mixed genesis
- Syndrome of intracranial hypertension

- Prematurity
- Iron deficiency anemia
- Intrauterine hypoxia
- (I'm not making these up.)

Here are some of the diagnoses for possible issues after birth:
- Residual cerebral insufficiency
- Psychomotor delay
- Physical delay
- Speech delay

MIKE: *There was no way of knowing if any of these diagnoses were accurate or reliable. For me, the biggest problem with all these possibilities was that I assumed that none of them were reliable or true. Only later, sometimes years later, did we realize that, yeah, some of them were.*

25. Toast for Lunch

Tuesday, August 17, 2004
Posted by Heidi

It's Tuesday. We survived the "informal meeting" from yesterday.

Mike continues to struggle with his stomach.

We visited the kids. When we arrived at 10:30, it was "outside time." We searched and found Nik right away. Where Meg ordinarily would be, she wasn't. The caregiver motions in another direction. Is it a different play area? We continue our search, going to each play area, and still no Meg. I begin to get concerned. We decide to go back inside to her room, and sure enough, there she is! A relief. For some reason they kept her inside. We don't know why. That took a good 15 minutes of our visit. The rest we spent outside. We've discovered another American couple working with a different agency who are adopting two young children. It was nice to converse with them.

This afternoon, we are invited by Theresa, the wife of the American family living here, to meet their staff and get a tour of their building. Also, they are having a special lunch for a couple on the staff and we are invited to stay.

In Kazakh tradition they toast (normally with shots of vodka) many times during whatever event they are celebrating. At this luncheon though, we had non-vodka beverages. First, the master of ceremonies speaks...we toast. Then, Mike and I are asked to stand and say some words. They were mostly of thank yous and hopes of getting to know them more during our stay. We toast. Then many others get up. We toast...and toast and toast again! It was a very nice

94

time. We are glad we stayed!

We were taken back to our hotel with only a few minutes to spare before heading back to the baby house. Mike leaves from the baby house with our driver to find some medication (Theresa gave him a prescription) and I stay with the kids. Meg and Nik were just getting up from naps and having a snack. I watched Meg shovel a huge chunk of bread into her mouth before the caregiver brought her to me. Meg then proceeded to choke (oh, no, not again!). After a long second, out came a nice handful of already-chewed bread. I had the bread in one hand and Meg's hand in the other as we walked to "the room." For some reason there are no trash cans visible in the baby home, so I bring a bag for trash with me each day and then dispose of it when we return to our hotel. In goes the bread.

Our visit went pretty smoothly after that. Meg and Nik mostly played independently of each other. I did spend quite some time holding Meg and, a couple of times now, she has come to me and turned her back to me so I can pick her up. A good sign. Meg had another "accident." I asked the translator to tell her, once again, that if she needs to go to the bathroom to tell Momma. Mike returned with the medication. 5:30 pm came and it was time to leave.

We are now back at our hotel. We hope the medicine will kick in soon for Mike so we can experience more of Taraz.

And so, with a toast to all of you, bye for today!

The Good Life: Amplify

Amplify is the fourth Element to living the Good Life.
It means expanding your Good Life to make it better.
I, Heidi tend to be a more introverted person, so being in
groups of people is not high on my list of fun things to do. That
being said, I did not want to pass up an opportunity to meet and
get to know people in Taraz, so we accepted the invitation. I had
no idea what to expect, but I was glad I pushed myself outside
my comfort zone.

I remember looking around the long table at all the people who
looked different and dressed differently from me, thinking, is this
real? I was in a foreign country, sitting with people I did not know
who spoke a language I did not understand while enjoying food I had
never seen! My nervousness faded and I was filled with gratitude to
be there in that moment. I enjoyed every minute of it!

MIKE: *It was awesome. It might have been the first time in our entire
trip that we felt positive.*

HEIDI: It was even nicer because Mike was getting some medicine.
Anxiety is heightened, knowing that something as minor as an illness
can seriously affect the adoption. Any bump or curve in the road was
cause for concern.

MIKE: *For some reason, I didn't write in the blog about the most
important event of all: how I procured some real medicine. It's a story
worth telling.*

Mike's trip to the neighborhood Kazakh pharmacy

*This illness was not going away. It made it hard to function normally
when, at a moment's notice, you find yourself racing for the
bathroom. I have no idea how I got through the "informal" meeting
or the visits. We brought stomach medications but they only worked
temporarily. The minute you sit up, the need for the bathroom hits.
You hope you can make it and then wonder if it is worth the walk
back to bed. By the third day I was desperate.*

*At the luncheon, Theresa told me I probably picked up a parasite,
most likely eating some local food. (Turns out, Theresa was a nurse.
Thank God!) She said Pepto Bismol wasn't going to get me healed up.*

It was important to get on some antibiotics. So she gave me a "prescription" and some directions written in Kazakh. While Heidi was with the kids, I showed our driver the directions.

I figured I'd be heading to some version of CVS, Drug Mart, or a similar pharmacy. After driving awhile, he pulls off the side of the busy road and puts the car in park. Then, he turns to me and motions across the road. I look. There is nothing there but a foreboding, decrepit apartment building. I point to the directions on the paper, and he nods and points to the scary building. I point to the directions again, and he nods again and smiles. Now, our driver seemed like a nice enough guy. But as I looked at him smiling, I thought, who is this little Kazakh man? He could be working for some version of the local mafia for all I knew (I have a great imagination). Here I was, an American, all alone. Was he sending me in to be robbed? Everyone outside of America believes all Americans are rich, right? I had a flashback to that first night at the airport.

Do I trust this guy?

After a few moments, I shrugged, opened the door, and scuttled across the busy two-lane road. I said a little prayer as I walked towards the building. I matched the number on the paper to the number on one of the doors.

This was not a Wal-mart pharmacy. It was basically a dark, single room with a man standing behind a counter. Behind him, I could see dozens, even hundreds, of little boxes of various sizes in a locked cage. I couldn't read the writing, of course, but I could tell that the printing on the boxes looked professional. Perhaps these were drugs and such.

I smiled awkwardly at the guy and handed him my little piece of paper. How in the world would this work, I thought? He looked at it, looked at me, then turned and unlocked the cage. After a few moments, he returned with a small box. No clue what was inside that box, but I was up for almost anything if it made me feel better.

I rubbed my thumb and fingers together and raised my eyebrows. Apparently, I guessed correctly at the universal hand symbol for "cash money." He wrote down a number on the same paper, and I paid him. When finished, I smiled and said, "Thank you" in Russian. He smiled back. I turned and headed back across the dusty road, feeling like a million bucks. I was so proud of myself for having navigated that international transaction. I was practically a diplomat!

Kazakh Tenge

The Good Life: Presence
Presence *is the final Element to living the Good Life.*
It means to thrive in your uniqueness.
Travel can make you feel amazing. I took a risk. And in the space
of ten minutes, I went from fearing a mafia-style hit to feeling
like the US Ambassador to the Republic of Kazakhstan. And, I
had drugs. Let the healing begin!

HEIDI: It was a pleasure to meet another couple going through the same adoption process. We mostly made small talk. Where are you from? How long will you be here, etc. Knowing we were not the only adoptive couple in the baby home was reassuring.

I finally located Meg and, within minutes, she was choking! My mind races. I need help! I need a witness! What if she chokes to death? What if I'm blamed? Where are the caregivers! And then, just like that, the huge chunk of bread is deposited into my hand. We calmly proceed to the music room as though nothing had happened.

I suspected Meg choked from eating too quickly because she didn't get enough to eat and she feared the food would be taken away from her. This can happen in institutional care. I did begin to wonder how many more life-and-death moments I would encounter with this little girl.

We were told when we first arrived that both Nik and Meg were potty trained. With Meg's several "accidents" already happening, I began to question the accuracy of that.

A once-in-a-lifetime luncheon, another near-death experience and a trip to a Kazakh "pharmacy." What a day! What, we wondered, could be next?

MIKE: Thus far, our adoption journey had been a lot like my stomach parasite problems: one uncomfortable, confusing, disorienting experience after another. We'd barely had a chance to get our bearings in a place (Almaty), and then we were whisked off to another unknown in this strange country (Taraz, in our spy car drive). From staring at the empty door, waiting for our first meeting, to The Apple Incident, and all the mania since, our time at this crossroads had been very hard.

The Good Life: Plot

In our hearts, we were crying out for some kind of normalcy. I don't think we ever really got that. But we kind of, sort of, had two adopted children now. They called us Momma and Poppa; we called them Nik and Meg. But nothing was official yet. And based on our experiences, I don't think any of us were really feeling like anything was guaranteed. We were moving forward at the crossroads. But it sure seemed like slow progress.

Questions to consider

"At the crossroads" is about Mike & Heidi making choices to move closer to their Good Life and away from their current life. What were some of the choices? What crossroads do you anticipate coming as you seek your Good Life?
*(For more questions and your **free** study guide,*
*go to **NotFar.org/Kaz)***

Part 3

...in the right

direction

26. Tipping Point

Tuesday, August 17, 2004
Posted by Mike

Recently, a book called *The Tipping Point* made its way around the business world. As I understand it, the term refers to the moment in time when a large number of seemingly small things add up to effect a significant change. Enough single drops of water will eventually spill a bucket. A tipping point.

Apparently, the author talks about several monumental changes that have occurred in the world, and he can isolate a specific day or even hour, when, finally, enough little things happened to make that historic change occur.

I'm saying all this to say that I think today was our tipping point in this adoption adventure.

Sunday was the hardest day. We were struggling, really missing our kids at home, feeling very strange in a strange land. Monday was the infamous "Informal Meeting." Of course, I, Mike, have been of little use to my wife, spending every spare moment sprawled on my bed, entirely convinced that the alien wallowing and churning within my stomach would pop out at any moment. Frankly, I would have welcomed it, if it would make me feel better.

So, why is today the tipping point?

Practically speaking, today is the exact midpoint for us. We have now been out of the US for two weeks. And we have two weeks left, including today. That by itself is enough to make us feel hopeful.

The antibiotics I began taking yesterday are slowly making a difference. For the first time in five or six days, I am able to function somewhat close to normal. If you've ever been this sick in a foreign environment, you know how hard everything—even the simplest things—becomes. It's obviously affected both of us. I'm looking forward to putting this behind me once and for all. ("Behind," get it? Come on, we need SOME juvenile humor here, right?)

This morning, both the kids displayed behavior we haven't seen much of before. We had Meg laughing. She was actually *laughing*. To say this is rare is a gross understatement. To see her smile and laugh today, we feel, was a huge step in this bonding process.

Nik also showed us some new parts of his personality. Thus far, he has been quiet, reserved, very mannerly and little "trouble." Today—wow. He has this very cute little smile. Today, he was trying to use that smile to deliberately do things we were saying "no" to. For the first time, we were seeing a real character! Suddenly, we both had visions of him racing through an airport— away from us. Or dropping food all over the floor. Or instigating a fight with a sibling. All with that cute little smile on his darling little face. How did that make us feel? "Our" little Nicky causing problems?

We say, it's about time.

It sparks the old parental instinct. It reminds us that there is a reason for parents in a child's life, and it's not just smiling sweetly and giving in to their whims. Oh, no. We relish the challenge. He doesn't know about his big brother Jake yet. And we're determined to have him understand what "no" means a LONG time before the two of them meet. Lord knows the disaster the two of them could wreak on northern New England otherwise!

It's good to begin to see the kids as who they really are. It's taken this long, and it's finally happening.

There is another reason, another factor in this tipping-point day. We believe, without a doubt, that, somehow, in some unexplainable way, the prayers of our friends and family have contributed. I may even go so far as to say that those are the hundreds of tiny drops that have made the difference for us.

We know it will continue to be challenging. We are still strangers in a strange land. It is very hot. We still have two weeks yet to go. We still miss our kids at home so much that just a flash of a memory can cause a lump in the throat and a stinging tear to be blinked back before anyone sees. But it is important for you to know that your thoughts and prayers are helping.

Spasiba, my friends. Thank you.

Postscript:

We ate lunch (Yes! I, Mike, had solid food!) here at the hotel today. (Although, unfortunately, it didn't stay around long!) We saw on the English menu "Kaappuccino."

Could it be...?

Thinking back to the wonderful cappuccini we savored in Almaty, we gave it a shot.

Now, how do I describe it? How about...thick, gelatinous, dark brown sludge with a light brown, sticky skin on its surface, tasting ever-so-slightly of burnt instant coffee with an expiration date of 1995.

When I get home, I may kiss the first Starbucks worker I see.

The Good Life: Power

*We made coffee in our room each morning with the small
French press we'd brought. Having our usual coffee routine,
even in such a foreign environment, was comforting. There's no
way we would have survived the hotel coffee, that's for sure!*

HEIDI: Knowing we were halfway through our time in Taraz marked a mental change. Also, Mike's improving health lifted my spirits. I began to feel that we were on the other side of difficulties we'd experienced so far. With two weeks behind us, we were, for the first time, able to see the light at the end of the tunnel.

New behaviors and interactions by Meg and Nik caused us to believe that progress was being made in our "bondation." We had no idea what Meg was capable of. We were concerned, based upon what we'd seen so far, that she might have limitations. Until this point Meg let me, and only me, hold her. She displayed little or no emotion except for crying. (We saw a lot of that!) If I set her down, she cried. If I gave her to Mike, she cried. It didn't seem fair that Meg's behavior was demanding my sole and complete attention, especially at Nik's expense. After all, I was Nik's momma, too! Just from a practical standpoint, it would not be possible for me to hold her every minute of every day!

A new strategy began during our visits. I intentionally gave Meg to Mike. Meg then displayed another emotion: anger! She squirmed out of Mike's arms, returning to me. I'd then scoop her up and return her to Mike. Eventually Meg, with blank face, allowed Mike to hold her for short periods of time.

MIKE: Oh, she loved that, I'll tell you. True daddy/daughter time (I say with sarcasm). I chose to tell myself she wasn't rejecting me, and that helped.

One of the hardest parts of adoption is not knowing "what you'll get." That may sound callous. But I bet I'm not the only adoptive parent who thinks it. Heidi would argue that you really aren't guaranteed anything with any child, whether biological or not, and she's right. However, I point out, you do know family history, and that counts for something.

With both of the kids, we had no information about their backgrounds. Yes, we had some rudimentary health records, but as we said, you couldn't count on those being true. So I spent a lot of my time watching the kids closely for signs of...I don't know, something. As Heidi said, with Meg, we were more concerned. She seemed emotionally flatlined. Well, except when she was crying non-stop. When she finally did laugh, it was a silent laugh. Kind of eerily sad, as if laughing was a skill she had never learned.

The Good Life: Presence
Adoption is the biggest "faith thing" I've ever done in my life. I've heard a phrase before: Love is a verb. As the author Bob Goff says, love *does*. And adoption, for me, was my biggest attempt to "do" love in my life (still is). It's an incredible feeling when you know you're "doing" your best. Everything feels...in sync.

HEIDI: Compared to our previous visits, seeing Meg laugh and respond to happenings around her was promising. It seemed Meg was beginning to relax, to let her guard down just a little. A relief!

There was one event where positive emotion came into play: eating! Mike and I brought food with us EVERY visit. We fed Nik and Meg ourselves. This was not because they couldn't feed themselves. For the first time in their lives Nik and Meg had a mother and father to feed them.

These two children had never been fed by a parent. Consider how sad that is. Both were eager and happy to eat each and every bite every time. I sometimes wondered if Meg's primary connection with me was in relation to food.

The power of breaking bread
We believe having meals with your kids (adopted or not) is important. Even if it's hectic or scattered or takeout, share the time to eat as a family. As parents of five grown children, we can look back and say without hesitation, it's worth it. Many of our best discussions happened around the table.

It's funny to read Mike calling Nik, "Nicky." We have not called him that since. Nik has always been Nik. We saw a mischievous charm that day that was delightfully adorable. We got a glimpse into the character of this child. Mike and I thought, hmmmm, this boy will be an interesting one to raise. There was a sense of eagerness in each of us to be THE parents to THESE children. We were ready to discover more of their character and personalities.

MIKE: Adoption was trusting that, no matter who these little strangers turned out to be...they would be my little strangers. My kids.

And, all these years later, I can quite honestly say they are my kids.

Adoption. What an amazing thing, huh?

27. Good Morning, Class

Wednesday, August 18, 2004
Posted by Mike

Today has gone by in a routine sort of way. The visit went well this morning. It was a lot cooler than yesterday. It was 97 when I checked at 7:30 last night, so I'm sure we were in the triple digits during the day. This morning was actually a bit cool—but then, 90 would feel cool in comparison. I seem to be on the upswing, illness-wise. Still struggling, but much better than a few days ago.

Before I get to the meat of this post, will you allow me a small rant?

I have two cell phones with me. I have a landline phone in my room. I have an MCI World Card with enough minutes to talk for ten straight hours. I have a "guaranteed" Kaz access number for that card. I have something called a Nursat Card, which can also be used to call anywhere in the world. Lastly, I have a new ACTIV card, which, again, grants calling anywhere *in the world*.

So, can someone tell me WHY I CAN'T MAKE ANY OF THEM WORK???

We have been here almost two weeks, and talked to our kids at home a total of five minutes. Why, oh why, can't I get a straight answer from anyone on the simple question I have: "Please, Sir, I'd like to call?"

This kind of thing drives me up the pickin' wall.

Leaf in a stream, Mike. Be a leaf in a stream.

Yes. A leaf that can't CALL HOME!!

Anyways...

Back in 7th grade world history, Miss Olex always had "compare and contrast" test questions. (Those tests were always over our heads. Once, she asked us to "make a generalization." The class almost rioted! Who knew what a "generalization" was?! We're twelve! She tried to give a specific definition to the generalization question, and then gave up.)

Here's an homage to Miss Olex:

Compare & contrast the two Kazakhstan cities of Almaty & Taraz
by Mike Vayda

Of course, given the small number of hours living amongst the good people of these cities, I realize this is quite irresponsible. (Guess I'll have to use a lot of generalizations!) Let's call it, "compare and contrast *in an ignorant manner.*"

Let's see. If Almaty is the New York of Kaz, then Taraz is...Detroit?

No. That, of course, is not fair. I haven't even been to Detroit. All I know about Detroit is that I hate the Pistons, wish Barry Sanders had not retired so early, and that Kiss had a cool song called "Detroit Rock City."

I guess I'll need to be less general.

Taraz is much smaller.

It is not nearly as cosmopolitan.

It feels more "foreign" than Almaty.

It does NOT make good cappuccino.

I'm told that Taraz is in the most "Kazakh" region of the entire country. As you may know (look out—here comes some history!), Kaz was one of the republics of the USSR. It has been attached to Russia even longer—since early in this century. Russia, sadly, has had her way with Kaz—really abused the environment, the natural resources, and much more.

The population of the country is very mixed. Many Russians came to help "settle" this land during Stalin's reign. You can see that mix in Almaty. Maybe there are more Caucasian than Asian? I can't say.

But the Russian influence is heavy there.

In Taraz, it looks and feels much more Asian; more Kazakh. We stand out here as we walk around.

This city is not booming like Almaty, but it is not economically depressed. Still, though, as we drive to the baby home, I see some similarities with other developing countries. I see cars here that I have only seen in movies from the early Sixties.

Temperature-wise, it is hotter and more arid than Almaty. We are near a river (although I can only find it on a map), so there are quite a few trees and much greenery here in the center of the city. The flowers are beautiful.

I'm pretty sure I'd choose Almaty if I had to make a choice. But we are very grateful to the people of Taraz for welcoming us here, and for the gift of two of their children.

For that reason alone, we will always consider Taraz a special place.

Okay, class. Wake up! The reward for your patience is the lifelong gift of learning that I have passed on to you today.

And remember, Reading is Fun-damental!

Oh, and if you see our Zack, Jake, and Brynn, please tell them we said "hi."

Because WE CAN'T!

HEIDI: Who knew it would be so difficult to call home. Not only were we exasperated that we couldn't get through to Zack, Jake, and Brynn, but so much of our time when not visiting Nik and Meg was spent trying to figure out this phone fiasco.

MIKE: It's amazing to me how different a world we lived in back in 2004. It's hard to believe we had to dial up the internet on a wired phone line. It took minutes to upload one picture. Quite often, the connection would be cut, and I'd have to start all over again. There was no Skype, no Facetime, no Zoom. We had email and the blog. And far too infrequently, a static-filled, fuzzy, blissful audio phone call with our kids back home.

At that time, I was on the cutting edge of tech. But my two cell phones and all my calling cards weren't working. It really was very frustrating.

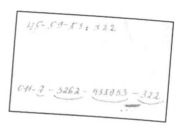

A few of our "phone notes" trying to find a solution

HEIDI: Not being able to connect with our family at home compounded our feeling of separation and isolation.

MIKE: Isolation. I agree. Things were going fine. But, man, did we feel alone. Sometimes at night, I'd lie there and wonder...what if something happened to one of the kids back home? What would we do? What could we do? Would we even hear about it?

Moments like that, lying there in the middle of the night, halfway around the world, was hard. I recall vividly those dark, quiet minutes, praying quietly and fervently. I was learning how little we can really control for our kids. And I was learning to let go and trust. It's hard to be a helicopter parent from a time zone 11 hours away—even if you wanted to!

HEIDI: Our exploration of the city up to this point consisted primarily of the car ride to and from the hotel and the baby home each day. And, of course, the view from our hotel window. My favorite spot was sitting at the window in our room. Watching life happen from above made me feel like I was part of Taraz. At least a little bit.

Taraz in mid-August was hot. Thank goodness for air conditioning in our room because that was the ONLY place that had A/C. The heat was a contributing factor to the tediousness of our daily visits. The "music room" was often stifling, especially in the afternoons. (OK, I admit it, Mike. You were right!) At first, we were not sure if we were allowed to leave the music room but boredom and high temperatures prompted us to take a chance and escape. Fortunately, we were not scolded and our visits began to include walks outside. This also gave Nik and Meg more to do and see. Some of the cutest pictures we have are of Nik and Meg as we strolled outside around the baby home.

MIKE: *When it was stifling.*

28. Missing the Weekend & Our Poor Girl

Friday, August 20, 2004
Posted by Heidi

Mike really wanted to spend today's post comparing and contrasting the Russian/Socialist political structure with the agricultural/nomadic traditions and the impact of both on today's Kazakh people. Fortunately, for you, I talked him out of it!

The last two days Meg has had a runny nose. Today, the nurse, through hand gestures, indicated that Meg has a slight fever. This explains why she was so hot and sweating yesterday and wanted to be held so much. I'm not sure, but I think the nurse was telling me she will give Meg medicine. Our translator only comes in the afternoon so it is a guessing game at this point.

Meg is quite thin, much thinner than Nik. I look forward to watching her body grow once she gets home. "Get some meat on those bones," as we say. Nik also seemed less curious and active. His nose has been a bit runny. We may have two sick kids over the rest of our stay here. Time will tell.

Other than that, our morning visit was uneventful.

Mike's cell phone has rung several times. He answers and it is a person speaking Russian or Kazakh. He says, "Wrong number...English...nyet." Over and over Mike replied when the phone rang. Finally we turned the phone off as we have no clue what else to say. We can't seem to get it to work, anyway, so why leave it on?

Being Friday, Mike and I would normally be looking forward to nachos and watching Tivo'd shows with Zack, Jake, and Brynn. And, oh yes, lattes on Saturday mornings (Mike makes a mean latte!) and German pancakes for late breakfast/early lunch! A glimpse into a weekend at the Vayda home (that's our other kids in the picture). As you can see, food is high priority. It's a change from the typical week. Here, there is little change from our weekly routine of seeing Meg and Nik twice a day and working anything else we do around that. We are okay with this routine except we miss weekends with our kids at home.

To all of you reading, have a fun weekend and stay healthy!

MIKE: *So our phone was ringing but, instead of it being our children, it was a stranger speaking a language we did not know. The irony!*

HEIDI: We were a bit worried when Meg wasn't feeling well.

How small were they?

For context, according to the Centers for Disease Control, at three years old, Nik was the weight of an average twelve-month-old in our country. The average weight for a three-year-old girl is 25-38 pounds. Meg weighed a mere 17.6 pounds, the weight of a nine-month-old baby!

I attributed their low weight to lack of proper food and nutrition. There could be other factors, such as sickness, parasites and disease.

MIKE: *You can tell how much we were jonesing for our weekend routine. I'd like to think that, if I had it to do over again, I would have spent more time outside of our little hotel room. I picture myself hanging out at the hotel bar, sipping Russian vodka martinis and charming the ex-Communists with my capitalist wit. But I need to give "2004 Mike" some grace. He was a sick puppy for many days. And those hot, boring-but-stressful visits to the baby home twice a day, including the 20-minute ride each way in an un air-conditioned car, really took a lot out of us. I don't recall feeling bored very often at the hotel. So, while I wish I had some exotic bar stories to tell you, the fact is, we never were the life of the party at the Hotel Zhambyl.*

I did go to the hotel bar once. It was after The Trial. I immediately ordered a vodka. I needed it. As you'll see.

29. M & H Phoned Home!

Saturday, August 21, 2004
Posted by Heidi

Methods of getting and giving medicine are different here. Meg is not feeling well, as I already posted. Yesterday afternoon the doctor came with a list of medicines for us to buy. Although Meg did not have a fever at that time, the doctor wanted us to purchase a list (in Russian) of three different medicines. Mike, along with our translator, went to a house/pharmacy (the same one he got his meds from). Mike delivered the medicine to the doctor, and she motioned for me to follow her with Meg. She led us to a room and we watched as another woman prepared the medicine...for an injection. She came over, needle in hand. Yup, antibiotics...by injection!

She plunged that inch-long needle into Meg's tiny bottom. And the loud scream that came out of Meg was long, as well. Next, medicine was squirted down the back of her throat. Meg gagged but it went down. She cried for awhile and I held her for the rest of our visit. The doctor said that the antibiotics—and that needle—will be given twice a day for five days! Poor Meg! I just said to myself, over and over again, "Be a leaf in a stream, be a leaf in a stream."

Regarding our phone saga, we asked Ildos, our translator, to help us see if our units were added and how many units we have to call the states. He called the Nursat Card number but, after one try, he said,

"I don't know...I don't know." It was clear he felt he had made an effort and he was done. When we got back to the hotel we tried on our own and fortunately figured it out. I anxiously waited until 7:45 am their time (6:45 pm our time) and got through! We talked with Zack and Brynn (Jake had spent the night at his cousin's house). Man, was it great to hear their voices! So, after over two weeks away, we have finally figured out a way to phone home.

A special thanks goes to Kevin, our brother-in-law, who made several attempts to help us figure this out. It is nice to know we have people in the states willing to try! Thanks, Kevin!

This morning's visit with the children was pleasant. Both Meg and Nik were happy and feeling all right. They played peek-a-boo behind a painted blue beam. The doctor seemed to say Meg had been given her medicine before we arrived. Who knows? I'll know more when Ildos comes.

Tonight marks our last two hours of 24. We are looking forward to the finale, even though Kim Bauer drives us crazy (we worry the rooms beside us hear us yelling at her). The show has been a welcome escape at the end of our emotionally draining days.

HEIDI: I was upset and angry once I recovered from the shock of watching Meg's injection. We were to buy the medicine, even though we didn't know what it was. We were not asked if we thought she needed medicine or how it should be given. Above all, I was bothered that I had no voice in what happened to her.

I didn't want Meg's first memories to be of me holding her down for a painful shot. I felt absolutely awful for her. Knowing she'd be going through this for the next five days didn't help, either. I reminded myself that our goal was to get these two little children home, so I kept my "eyes on the prize" instead. It stirs up the emotions, though, even today!

MIKE: How discouraging when Ildos, our only contact, a native to Taraz, could not (or would not) figure out our phone problems. Or at least find someone who could. Would we ever be able to get through to our kids at home? He was a nice young man. I wonder if age had something to do with his reticence. Boy, was I thankful for Kevin's efforts in helping us figure this out! I can't even remember the specifics now. But to finally, after over two weeks, get through was a victory. It felt good knowing he and my sister Melissa were so connected to us half a world away. Anything to make us feel less isolated was welcome.

A gift that kept on (not) giving
I spent a lot of money buying phone minutes and loading them
onto our MCI World Calling Card. I never used one of them in
Kaz. For years, I carried that dang card with me trying to use
those minutes. I eventually gave up.

HEIDI: Knowing our kids were alive and well meant everything. Talking with six-year-old Brynn, I thought about how much her world was going to change. Instead of being the third child and only daughter, she would soon be the middle child and become a big sister for two siblings. Meg would now be the youngest daughter. Lots of changes coming.

MIKE: We brought the DVD set of 24 season one with us. At that time there was no other reliable means of watching entertainment in a developing country. It's funny, I don't think I even turned on the TV once while we were there. Normally I like to learn more about the local culture, but I guess we'd had enough exposure with everything else that was going on. Media was for escape, not reinforcement of how foreign things were.

HEIDI: Finding a way to decompress from the stress and discomforts of each day was necessary. *24* was a great escape. I have to admit I was the one begging, "Come on, let's just watch one more!" Mike, being the sensible one, said we needed to pace ourselves or we'd have nothing to watch later. "Yeah, but just one more?!?"

MIKE: *I think we "escaped" an appropriate amount. We were stressed out! We didn't smoke. Didn't drink. Didn't chew. We 24'd.*

Meg almost wasn't "Meg"

We almost changed Meg's name because of *24*! We loved the character of Nina. She was awesome! Smart, pretty, and a great name. Maybe it was my stomach parasite talking, but I, Mike, actually suggested renaming our new daughter Nina instead of Meg. Heidi wasn't opposed to the idea. And then we got to the end of the season.

Let's just say, we're happy we stuck with "Meg."

30. Gypsies, Tramps & Thieves

Monday August 23, 2004
Posted by Mike

(Bad news! Heidi is trying valiantly to fight off a stomach illness. We're praying it's not the same thing I had. Montezuma in Kazakhstan was supposed to have taken the train out of town a few days ago—right, Zack?)

Anyone know why I chose the post title? Does anyone remember that song by Cher? (Anyone? Anyone? Please, someone tell me I'm not all alone in the '70s.) It came out when I was, maybe, ten. I remember my cousin Lori and me singing it rebelliously. Of course, we didn't have a clue what it meant, but it all sounded so mysterious.

Today we were having lunch outside at the hotel restaurant and that song came on. It was pretty funny to hear it again after all these years...and to hear it in Taraz, Kazakhstan made it surreal.

Thinking back to when I used to sing that song with my cousin, could I ever have dreamed of this? Of me, here, halfway around the world? Adopting two children? Funny how life takes you places you never intended or dreamed of when you were young.

I, for one, am glad I am here. It tells me two things:

First, I've not shied away from challenges. I am, even past 40, being stretched beyond my zone of comfort. Sure it's hard, and a bit scary. But man, what if all I'm living my life for is to continuously seek comfort and security? This sure has shaken me out of that mindset. I think that raising these kids will be a steady reminder through the years of what really does matter.

Second, it tells me that even I, a fairly selfish person, can do something for somebody else. Although I've never had a burning desire to adopt, I clearly see how this choice will make a difference for Good in the world.

Maybe it's because I'm getting old(er). But I am thinking much more about the impact—the "dent"—I am leaving on this world. I won't have a hit song that is still played in Taraz 30 years later like Cher. But I believe that, because of our choice now, the world will be improved, a small fraction, for all time.

That makes me feel pretty good.

We took a day off from posting yesterday and spent our free afternoon with the Americans (the folks we told you about earlier). We had a great lunch and a nice relaxing afternoon of discussion and community. It was so much better than last Sunday, when we were feeling very alone. The kids running through the house screaming and slamming doors sure made us feel right at home!

Here's an interesting picture of one of Nik's caregivers from Saturday. It was so hot, and Nik's group was allowed to go play in the "pool" (it's really nothing more than an oversized birdbath). I like the picture so much because the caregiver began outside the pool, then rolled up her pant legs to step in and play a little with the kids, then finally just dove right in! It was really fun to watch her. The kids were  climbing all over her, laughing and screaming.

This picture shows her interacting with Nik, but it could have been any of the kids. She really loves them. It encourages me to see someone give so much unselfishly. It gives me hope.

This is a great picture of Meg, with a wonderful smile on her face.

She's looking at Heidi, who, I think, is playing patty-cake with her. She still doesn't smile a lot, but we've seen a change in her...a real positive change. (Heidi and I have a difference of opinion on the song. I was raised to sing it as "Patty cake," while Heidi is sure it's "pat-a-cake." Thankfully, it does the trick both ways.)

Nik? Well, you can see from the picture that he's still a character.

The final picture is of the kids in Meg's group. Every day, all of them come running up to shake my hand. They're all smiles and really a joy to see. So I thought, maybe, as a conclusion to all this serious conversation, they'd give you a smile, as well.

(I especially like the one on the far left who's waving).

MIKE: *Our kids in Maine read our posts. I mentioned Zack in the post because, on the phone, he was very confused about who this guy Montezuma was, and how we knew him!*

HEIDI: Mike wrote: "What if all I'm living my life for is just to continuously seek comfort and security? This sure has shaken me out of that mindset." Adoption is not for the fainthearted. For us, adding Nik and Meg to our family has been a continual process of discovery. Without personal history or family history we constantly wonder and try to understand who they are and what they need in every situation. This has kept us on our toes.

Our brain is primarily imprinted in the first three years of life. This fact is sad for Mike and me. We were not able to be the loving parents from the start for Nik and Meg. This is something that every child deserves. We can't undo the impact of living in institutional care, either, but we can try to positively influence their lives moving forward.

The Good Life: Amplify

Adopting Nik and Meg into our family has been our attempt to, as Mike said, improve the world a small fraction, for all time. Their futures are not up to Mike and me. But we did give two little beings an opportunity. We believe that is one step closer to good in this world.

MIKE: *To this day, looking at Nik and Meg's faces reminds me how the Vayda Family chose a different path than most. Sometimes I wish I could crawl inside their minds and know how secure they feel now.*

We came to the conclusion that Nik was probably a favorite in the baby home. He had a charming amiability with the caregivers and it seemed to be reciprocated.

Nik is definitely a people person. We think that was a coping trait for him. For Meg, it seems that self-preservation was her way to survive. We saw evidence of that all through her growing up. We often cautioned her not to assume the worst about people, to give them a chance before deciding they were out to get her.

Baby homes. What a hard place to learn how to be a child!

HEIDI: I learned that parents unable to care for their children in Taraz can temporarily leave their child in a baby home or orphanage. The parents must visit regularly or they will lose their parental rights. That means that some of those kids weren't in line for adoption. At least, at first. It strikes me that this was both a baby home and, in a sense, a foster home.

Children in groups of eight or so would often pass by us when we were outside. We'd give big smiles, causing many of these little ones to come over and put out their hands for us to shake. Mike and I were thrilled to make eye contact and shake their hands whenever we could. We hoped they might sense our love for them.

MIKE: I felt responsible to give every child I came in contact with some kind of encouragement. I look at those pictures and wonder, where are those dear kids now? I hope it's someplace safe and good. I really hope. As I write this, another generation is in that baby home. And on and on it goes.

A way to help!
Many of our discussions with our American friends were about the needs of the children in the baby home and orphanages. From these discussions, we started a sponsorship program. It allowed our family to help support two children until they left the orphanage. It was a great reminder to all of us where Nik and Meg could have been.

31. Apparently, it Does Take a Village

Tuesday, August 24, 2004
Posted by Mike

This morning we were wondering why the A/C wasn't coming on. I turned it all the way to 11. Still no air. "Huh. Maybe we should open the window...?" So we did.

It couldn't be. It was COOL outside. I mean, honest to goodness cool. It has been so hot here. Like, Africa hot. The one saving grace is that it does cool off quite a bit in the evening. And during the day, as long as you are in the shade, you can tolerate it. But the sun is brutal.

It was so refreshing to feel that crisp, clean air come in (although, since we're right over the city's main intersection, I can't vouch for the "clean" part).

Our visit this morning went well. We try to spend the morning visits outside. By now, you all know how much we LUUVV the music room. If ever there was a room that was crying out for a ceiling fan, this is it. So, this morning in particular was fantastic. It was cute to see a lot of the kids bundled up.

You know, keep off the chill...

I may have mentioned this (in the "don't dare sit on the bare concrete" episode), but children really are public property here. Everybody has an opinion. And we've been truly blessed to hear so many of these opinions. What's that you say? How do we know what they're saying if they speak Kazakh? Oh, they are very good at pantomime. And if you don't understand, they'll keep at it until you do!

Just the other day, I was outside with Nik and a well-dressed woman walks past us towards the front door of the baby home. I nod and smile tentatively. She glances at Nik, says hello (I think), then does a double take. She stops dead in her tracks, walks over, looks intently at him, then goes into a different door. Speaking Kazakh all the while.

A moment later, she comes back out with a dish towel and proceeds to THOROUGHLY wipe Nik's nose. What did Nik do? He stood there patiently and let her, of course.

Apparently, it DOES take a village to raise a child.

We are trying not to worry about the court date. I have started to think of it as "The Trial." Today officially marks two weeks of bonding (one week left; woo-hoo!), and our facilitator officially petitioned the court for a date of 8/31. The plan is to leave immediately after court, that night, for Almaty. We would arrive Wednesday morning, and fly out on the very next flight, which is Wednesday night. (Actually, it's Thursday. But when the flight leaves at 3:30 am, and you leave for the airport at 1:00 am, who's counting?)

Now, if that court date slips by even one day, we're stuck. Using frequent flier miles to get us here was a huge blessing and $$ savings. The only downside is it will be near impossible to change our return date. Worst case? We'd have to buy two last minute tickets, and maybe not get out of here for several more days. So, it's an exercise in faith to not let our minds wander over to that area of our thinking and begin to bite our nails. Cause we *reeeally* want to get home. But, overall, I think we're doing a pretty good job of being leaves. (You know, in a stream.)

We learned a lot about our status yesterday.

Our facilitator, who speaks English, chose to instead speak Kazakh to our interpreter. They began having a conversation at 5:45 pm and finished up around 5:51 pm. We stood patiently during the long conversation, watching their expressions, trying to intuit what was being said.

Finally, when they finished, we asked Ildos what they talked about. *For God's sake, how is everything?!*

"She said that things are fine."

"So, that's all she said?"

"Yes."

"So, things are...going well?"

"Yes. Fine."

I kid you not.

Our interpreter. A man of few words.

HEIDI: We look back and laugh about all the advice and instruction we received from the staff. At the time, it was difficult, though. We didn't want to do anything wrong or improper against their ways and culture, but inevitably we did. Sometimes we figured out the problem and other times we had no idea.

The Good Life: Plot
The more those situations happened, the more we talked about our own strategies for what our new life would look like. We couldn't wait to get home with Nik and Meg. We just needed to be patient a few more days.

Galina, our facilitator, was our only source of information regarding our adoption proceedings. What she had to say was really important to us. We hung on her every word. Her English was limited, so sometimes we wondered if we understood her correctly. If Ildos was available, he would translate.

Ildos attended most of our visits with Nik and Meg. He sat off to one side unless we had questions or needed help. At first, it felt awkward with someone watching all the time, especially since everything was new to us.

A nagging doubt
Was he *really* a translator? Or could he be an informant? Was he there to decide if we were qualified to adopt? Of course he wasn't an informant. But remember we were constantly told about the dangers around us. It played tricks with our minds.

Ildos was also available for other translation needs such as the market, hotel, pharmacy, and restaurants. (Phone? Not so much.) He taught us Kazakh words and phrases (see photo) that were of help when we were on our own. As time went on, Mike and I became more comfortable around him and that warmth was reciprocated.

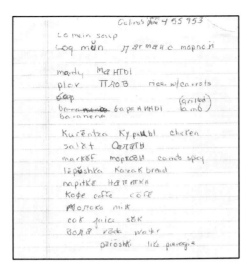

Some of Heidi's attempts at translations. Also, Galina's phone number, which, of course, we couldn't figure out how to call, no matter how many attempts were made.

MIKE: He may have been a fine translator (how would we ever know, anyway?!). He was young; about twenty-one or so. It would have been nice to have a translator with a better rapport with children. We made the most of our situation, though. Ildos was a nice guy, and we're thankful for how he helped us learn about the Kazakh culture.

We hardly ever saw Galina while in Taraz. When we did see her, we'd try to pry any information we could out of her in our short interactions. And then to hear the translation, "Things are fine," was just too ridiculous. As a businessman, I couldn't help but wonder how much it cost me to have our interpreter there at all times, every day.

If he got paid by the word, he made a fortune.

32. It's Showtime...at the Baby Home!

Wednesday, August 25, 2004
Posted by Heidi

At Nik's play area there was a performance.

Several staff were in attendance, including the director. We were offered seats right away. One caregiver played the accordion while the second caregiver guided the children through their routines. There was a relay race, an obstacle course, tug-of-war, and ring-around-the-rosey. The play area was decorated with hanging miniature inflatable balls (which Mike and I had given them), and the children had hand bells and horns to add to the music. The kids had so much fun!

Nik's group has great kids in it. Nik did not participate much and began crying so they let him come sit with us. We were told that, if the parents are there, the child will often cry. I am not sure why that is, but that's the explanation we received. Mike asked to take a picture of his group when the show was over. That took some doing for the two caregivers, but they were gracious and we got a couple shots.

The best was saved for last: a cake was brought out and, at that point, you could have heard a pin drop! Each child got a piece (including Meg and Nik). The cake was thoroughly enjoyed! Impromptu entertainment was a pleasant change from our typical morning visits.

Nik's group and caregivers

Yesterday Mike and Ildos and I went to an Uzbek Restaurant. Uzbekistan is the country just south of Taraz and many Uzbek live here. We had *lug mun* and *plouf*. The lug mun is like a soup with meat, chives, and very thick homemade noodles. It is really good. Plouf is a type of rice with carrots and beef. That also is tasty. I only ate the lug mun along with bread because of my stomach. It was a test to see how it would settle. My stomach failed miserably and I paid for it the rest of the day. Today I called Theresa, our nurse friend, and she told me what medicine to get at the pharmacy. We were able to get it and I began taking it right away, and will for five days. Hopefully that'll do the trick.

How many times did they get cake like this?

Galina told us our documents have been given to the court. I believe we are waiting for the court date. Maybe we will find out today.

Maybe not. :)

HEIDI: Watching the children perform and having fun was a joy for us. The show that culminated in cake eating was the best! How often do the children get cake? I wondered.

"Children often cry when parents are there." Hmmmm. I remember being surprised that Nik, who was typically more social, cried, rather than participating. Is there some kind of worry or concern for these children when their prospective adoptive parents are around?

The Good Life: Be

MIKE: I studied the faces of those dear children while they were "performing" for us. Were there other American parents who came for them after we left? Were there other performances in celebration? Was there sadness when they returned to their rooms, knowing they were not "chosen" like Nik and Meg? Life is so unfair.

None of those children—not one—deserved to be orphaned. For those few moments, that little cake brought them all such joy. I wonder if we paid for the cake in some roundabout way? I sure hope so.

Lug mun and Plouf! The Uzbek dishes were so good!

I'm pretty sure our stomach issues were food related. Once Mike was in recovery, I was hit with "the revenge." I knew the protocol and immediately contacted Theresa who rescued me from prolonged misery! Thank you, Theresa!

Deciding what and if we should eat during our time in Taraz was always a tough call. We settled on only eating local food when we knew we could return directly to our hotel, juuuust in case.

Lug mun (above) and Plouf. So good!

Our luggage was weighed down with PowerBars on our flight to Kazakhstan. I packed all three flavors, chocolate, peanut butter, and vanilla. They were a staple in our diet for weeks.

Who Needs Diets?

Peanut butter cups are one of my (Heidi) favorites. Sometimes for a "special" treat I'd layer the chocolate and peanut butter flavors together, creating my own peanut butter cup, of sorts. International adoption, an alternative weight loss solution!

33. Aisha Bibi, Baby!

Thursday, August 26, 2004
Posted by Mike

Today we broke out of our routine and went to visit every single tourist attraction in Taraz.

Yes! Both of them.

They are mausoleums (a building for an expired person). One of them is right here in town. Actually, there are two mausoleums in one park. One of them is purposely built crooked. It is said the reason why is so that the king who is buried there will have no rest in the afterlife. Apparently, he was a pretty nasty ruler.

The other mausoleum in the park is for a man named Karakhan. Let's leave him for a moment and talk about the second tourist attraction, which is about twenty minutes out of town: the mausoleum built for Aisha Bibi.

Aisha Bibi (a lot of fun to say; g'head, give it a try!) was a beautiful woman who was in love with a man that she was forbidden to date. Or court, or email, or whatever they did 2,000 years ago for dating. They arranged to secretly meet outside of town, but she was bitten by a snake and died before they could be together. The man who loved her? Happened to be Karakhan, whom we mentioned a few sentences ago. He built her a beautiful resting place. It really is stunning. It is enclosed within Plexiglas walls now to try and protect it from the elements.

As Paul Harvey used to say, the rest of the story is that, when Karakhan died years later, he had his mausoleum built in the city. BUT, it is said that, if you climb high enough, you will see that his resting place is in a direct line of sight, all the way out to Aisha Bibi's. He wanted them to be able to see each other for all eternity.

So, kinda cool, eh?

And it is a LOT of fun to say her name. Aisha Bibi!

The afternoon visit with the kids went pretty well. Today it seemed like Meg really came out of her shell. It's like she was exercising her new confidence or something. Up till now, she had spent all or nearly all of our visits in Heidi's arms. Today, she was strutting her tiny little body up and down the music room like she owned the place. It was great to see.

And Nik actually said, "Buh bye" today. It was hugely cute. That's mah boy—proud to be an English speaking Amurican!

Of course, no word on our court date. It would do no good to press them on this. That much is obvious. So, we'll try and show all of you how much faith we have that all will work out for good in the end. We just kinda hope it will all work out for good in the end on TUESDAY.

Next week at this time (court date permitting, of course), we'll be saying "Buh bye" ourselves and on the plane to Amurica. Looking way, way forward to that.

And, as I gaze across the long distance between our twin beds, to *my* little Aisha Bibi, I bid all of you a good day.

— NOW —

HEIDI: Breaking out of our routine with our tour of Taraz in the morning and then visiting Nik and Meg just in the afternoon made for an enjoyable day. Karakhan and Aisha Bibi, isn't that a beautiful story?

Sarah, another American friend who works with Dave and Theresa, was gracious enough to be our guide. Having lived in Taraz for several years, she knew a lot about the area. Mike and I may not have seen so many of the sights if it were not for her. Thank you, Sarah!

MIKE: I really enjoyed that trip out and about. I wish we had done so much more. Our American friends were a Godsend. It was such a lucky thing (a grace thing) that we even knew they were there!

How we met our friends
Right before we left, I stumbled on a blog written by some Americans who just got back from adopting in Taraz. I reached out to them (from Taraz), and they connected us with Dave and Theresa. Interestingly, we ended up moving to Ohio and living not very far away from the bloggers.

Man, if we hadn't met them...would we have survived? I suppose so. But we would've been miserable. We might have had to find a hospital or a doctor. And wouldn't THAT have been an experience with our interpreter? Just imagine going to a hospital in another country like Kazakhstan. Would our insurance cover it? Would we have to pay cash? Not to mention the quality of care is a complete unknown. Thank God. Seriously.

HEIDI: It was fun seeing Nik and Meg acting more like three year olds and for Meg to participate instead of being held.

Every day we hoped for news of our court date and every day that went by with no information was discouraging. We very much hoped the saying, "no news is good news" would ring true in this situation.

MIKE: As the late, great Tom Petty would say, the waiting was the hardest part. We were dying to know if we would be leaving as planned. So much was riding on it. Last-minute plane tickets would cost a fortune. In hindsight, all that thinking about leaving may have kept me from dwelling on the actual court date, at least somewhat.

Good thing I didn't know what was in store for us at court!

34. Maybe, Maybe Not

Friday, August 27, 2004
Posted by Heidi

Our facilitator is leaving for the weekend but, before leaving, Mike decided to ask her one more time about court. She said we are scheduled for 3 pm on Tuesday. That was surprising additional information. This may be good news.

We are not sure.

Maybe, maybe not...

Our morning visit went smoothly. In the morning, we usually walk around the baby house a few times and then sit on an outside bench until Meg and Nik leave for lunch. We've already mentioned that kids are public property. I typically hold Meg as we walk. I think it is good for our bonding and her security. As we walked, one of the passing staff began talking to Meg and to our translator. Just what I thought; we were informed Meg should walk, not be held.

Okay! I put her down and she walked the rest of the way to the bench. I asked the translator why. "Because Meg will learn to expect to be held." Things like this just make me long to be home so we can begin to parent in our own way.

I know, "leaf in a stream."

We just returned from visiting one of the older orphanages in Taraz with Sarah, our American friend. Her employer sponsors three groups of children and we had the opportunity to meet many of them. I'm glad we had the chance to go!

It was so cute yesterday when Nik said, "buh bye" to us. Mike and I were surprised! He said it perfectly and then kept saying it to me and waving as Mike took him down the hall to his group. This morning we said "Hi" to him and he said "Hi" back and waved. He was so cute! Again! It is great to hear him picking up some of what we are saying. Hopefully soon, Meg will, too. She never says a word with us, although Meg's caregiver says she is very talkative in her group. Hmmm.

We happened to see the other adoptive couple at the baby house. We hadn't seen them in a long time. They had court yesterday. They said it went well and pretty easily. I am sure they are relieved. One more step done in their process. We are very happy for them!

Tonight we have been invited to David and Theresa's house for movie night again. We are looking forward to that. I think they will have pizza too. MMMM, PIZZA! This just reminds me that, if all goes well, next week at this time we could be having movie night with Zack, Jake, and Brynn. I am REALLY looking forward to that!

We spoke with our oldest son Zack last night and also to my mother, Barbara. Good once again to hear their voices. Zack told Mike on the phone that he is proud his parents are doing something so brave. Mike told him the whole Vayda family is doing something brave—Zack, Jake, Brynn, as well as Nik and Meg. It's a bit of a struggle to remain patient through these final six days, though. We need to keep focused on this "brave thing." We'll all make it. :)

HEIDI: Mike and I finally figured out through our own process of deduction that Galina stayed in Taraz during the week and returned to Almaty on the weekends. I don't know why she couldn't have just told us that.

MIKE: But honestly, we really didn't see her much. At all. I could have used some more "facilitating" throughout the entire process. I don't see why we needed to feel so alone. We tried to just accept it, but, as we've said many times, it wasn't easy.

HEIDI: The court date? Three o'clock on Tuesday it is. By this time, we were skeptical it was going to happen.

The Good Life: Plot

"Meg should not be held." By that point, I was eager to make my own decisions on what was best for her. I was feeling more and more confident that I was ready to be Meg's mom. And I couldn't wait to get started.

The orphanage we toured for older children was quite sparse and sterile. Even so, the kids were smiling and friendly. Many of the children had disabilities. I wondered, as we were walking through the place, would this have been Nik and Meg's next "home?"

MIKE: Man, we jumped at the chance to hear how the other couple's court date had gone. They were just ahead of us in the adoption process so we were getting the inside scoop. Even though they weren't working with the same agency as us, we relied on their experience as a gauge for ourselves. It was good news that their court date went smoothly. We thought, why should ours be any different?

The Good Life: Amplify

HEIDI: The adoption of Nik and Meg was a family affair. We included Zack, Jake, and Brynn all along the way. We talked of how adoption would change our family. We were adding two children who needed a family. It would be hard, but were we, as a family, willing to be "brave?" Yes.

Zack, Jake, and Brynn sacrificed being away from their parents. So for Zack, an eleven year old, to say he was proud of his parents in the midst of our separation was exceptionally meaningful!

MIKE: It was a stroke of lucky brilliance (more grace!) that Heidi and I included our three children as active members of the adoption mission from the beginning. It helped so much in the days and years after. Instead of having two separate groups of children, we truly do have a family. Of course, that evolved over time and with a lot of effort. But having our kids buy into the family mission from the very beginning was so important.

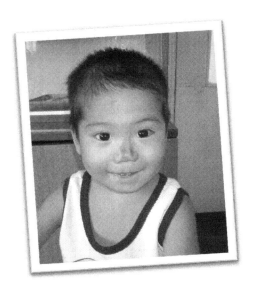

35. Snow Day!

Saturday, August 28, 2004
Posted by Mike

Last night we had an enjoyable evening again with our American friends. Heidi made an absolute pig of herself with the pizza. Just kidding. She only had eight pieces. But the best news we received was yesterday during our visit. No visit this afternoon. We have a "snow day!"

This may sound cold-hearted, but hear me out. It can be tiring seeing the kids two times each day. It's not the kids that are the issue; it's seeing the kids in that environment. We've already regaled you with the "it takes a village" philosophy of raising kids here, how everybody has an opinion and feels compelled to share it. Being at the baby house really restricts you from beginning to parent in the way you want. It's nobody's fault. They have a system that is amazing in its efficiency. The facility is clean, well-managed, and the children genuinely seem to enjoy their little world. However, it is, of course, still an orphanage. And here we are, two foreigners, trying to begin our lives with two of the 150 children. It really is a clash of agendas more than a clash of cultures.

Afternoons are the hardest. Usually it is very hot, so we can't spend much time outside. The beloved music room is stifling in the lack of circulation (Hey! Did I ever tell you it was stifling?) Toys are extremely limited. There is a lot of crankiness and whining because it is late afternoon.

And the kids can complain, too.

So, when I tell you that we decided NOT to go to the afternoon visit today, you'll understand that we're jumping up and down with glee because of the situation, not because of the lack of face time with Nik and Meg.

This came about because we were discussing how to begin the "leaving." How do you have the kids understand that we'll be going away for several weeks—especially when we've been coming every day, twice a day, for several weeks? And, on top of that, when we come back, "we" won't be coming. Poppa will be staying at home, and instead, Apa (Grammie) will be coming with Momma?

Our translator said that previous parents began to reduce their visits towards the end. At the close of the morning visit, they would explain to the children that Momma and Poppa had some very important things to do, and would not be back until tomorrow. This would begin to ease them into the upcoming big change.

So, we did just that this morning. The kids seemed to really be listening to our translator. It was interesting to see them concentrating. Tomorrow, we'll tell them for the first time that we'll be leaving in a few days for a long time.

Will they "get it?" Who knows, really? We do know that the entire baby house is aware of this adoption. Indeed, it seems that Nik and Meg are the rock stars of the whole place. Everywhere we walk, kids and even caregivers call out their names. So, in addition to feeling pretty darn good with all the attention, it seems that the kids are getting clear and repeated reinforcement about how their world is going to change.

Do they understand just how thoroughly their world will be rocked? At age three, I doubt it. I do know that they both seem to really be opening up to us over the past few days. Meg is strutting all over the place with a little smirk on her face. Nik is now confident enough with me to be "chased"; his little body will waddle all over the room, screaming with laughter as I try to catch him. So, in the end, you keep doing what you've been doing all along. You go on faith that they'll be ready *enough*.

And we'll enjoy the afternoon off. After all these visits, it feels exactly like an unexpected snow day felt when we were school kids.

Now, about the picture of Nik above. I mentioned how the kids are rock stars here. Well, they were walking with Heidi and one of the caregivers reached down and gave Nik a big kiss. He walked back into the room where I was, and I saw red all over his nose. He had this silly look on his face. I thought, "Oh man he's BLEEDING!" Heidi walked in and laughed.

It's just lipstick.

HEIDI: The pizza and the company made for a fun and comforting Friday night. We couldn't have asked for a better evening out.

Having a "snow day" for the reasons Mike stated was an unexpected pleasure. It was especially so because it was the beginning of the end. Our time in Taraz was winding down and we welcomed the next phase.

We were concerned that Nik and Meg wouldn't understand our departure. We prepared them as best we could but the uncertainty of their grasp on the situation remained.

The picture of Nik with the lipstick is a favorite. The look on Nik's face and the spontaneous evidence of a loving caregiver means a lot.

MIKE: *In the blog post, I ruminated on whether the kids had any idea of what was about to happen. If you ask Nik and Meg what they remember about their first three years of life—including the actual adoption process—they'll say...nothing.*

Nothing!

They remember zero about Kazakhstan. It's so hard to believe. We write a whole book, and they remember nothing. Good thing we have the book, huh?

My Duru Lady
We had some fun trying to recreate our favorite (and only) soap in Taraz, *Duru Lady*. I think she could be a model, don't you?

36. Bizzee Bazaar

Sunday, August 29, 2004
Posted by Heidi

After visiting the kids yesterday morning, our translator agreed to take me to the bazaar. The bazaar is the place where everyone goes to buy stuff. I wanted to purchase the same potty chair that the kids have at the baby home, and some shoes similar to what they wear now. Our American friends will let me store a few items with them until my return. I was told this weekend is the absolute worst time to go as school begins next week. But it was the only day available.

Each vendor has an enclosed stall. There are also some small stores. The stalls are right beside each other with a sidewalk width of space for people to walk. Stalls are on either side as you walk. There is some pushing in the crowd. Our translator warned me to watch my money as there

are many thieves here. The stalls go on and on...it's huge! Our translator says the definition of bazaar is disorganized, crowded, and loud talk. That does sum it up.

We went before noon before it got too crowded and hot. It did not take us long to find the items I was looking for and we left. I had been wanting to see what it was like. I'm glad I got to experience the bazaar. For some strange reason, especially knowing Mike is the "shop till you drop" kind of person, he didn't want to go!?!

After I got back we went to see our American friends. We got back around 8 pm, in time to watch 24 and head to bed. It was a full day even without seeing Nik and Meg in the afternoon.

Oh, and here's the BEST news of all: turns out our friends were given *season two* of 24 by a previous adopting couple. Can you believe it! Of all the DVDs out there, they had the one we were watching. We were thrilled to borrow it! Of course, now we have to finish and return it before our departure!

Today's visit was nice. Nik continues to say, "hi" and "buh-bye." We have been experimenting with giving different types of food to the kids lately. Three days ago Mike held out a chocolate PowerBar to Nik and Meg and it was gone in two or three bites! Today Mike took a different approach by breaking off small pieces. They both stood quiet and attentive, just waiting for their next piece. Zack, Jake, and Brynn...remember eating PowerBars in France last summer?

I tried individual size yogurts with them a few days ago and that went well so I brought a pint of yogurt yesterday and they ate the whole thing! Wow! I guess that's a winner. You can see Meg's greedy expression in the picture above.

Our driver's car broke down on his way to get us this morning so he came with a backup car. After our visit he drove us to a restaurant and dropped us off, along with our translator. We'd heard the restaurant had good Georgian food (as in Georgia the country, not Georgia the state). It was closed, and our driver had already left!

So instead we went to a Turkish restaurant and ordered doners (meat cooked on a spit type thing) and pizza. We had a bit of a walk but it worked out fine. We ordered more than enough so we'd have leftovers for tonight in the hotel. All the food was good. Sometimes for a vegetarian pizza, they put peas on it, too. Interesting, huh? It has been great to eat the last few days without having to pay for it later!

Tomorrow is Monday, and maybe we'll find out more about our court date scheduled for Tuesday. Then again, maybe not!

HEIDI: Clothes are communal in the baby home so Nik and Meg had no belongings of their own. Everything Nik and Meg would need (clothes, diapers, toys, medicine, food, etc.) for the trip home I had to bring myself. Once I knew their approximate sizes I could purchase clothes and shoes. I thought it would be comforting for Nik and Meg to have items that looked familiar to them. Meg was definitely not potty trained (even though they assured us she was) and, even if she was, neither of them were able to sit easily on a regular toilet seat so I bought two plastic potty chairs like the ones they used in the baby home.

I found the bazaar fascinating and frustrating. Crowds are not my favorite thing and I am not a big shopper. I did manage to get what I was looking for and escaped with my wallet intact.

MIKE: *I know, I know. I should have gone to the bazaar. It was a cultural experience and all that. I fully enjoyed the cultural nap I had instead.*

HEIDI: Those sticky, gooey PowerBars are not a two or three bite kind of bar! Nik and Meg practically inhaled the food. We'd have many more choking sessions on our hands if we'd left them to their own devices. Yes, Nik and Meg ate a whole pint of yogurt in one sitting!

We definitely enjoyed all the varied culinary cuisines, especially now that it stayed in our stomachs. From Turkish to Uzbeki to Kazakh pizza and traditional Kazakh horse, of course. It was a pleasure to experience so many unique dishes.

Travel is a tug-of-war
We believe nothing changes a person like travel (except tragedy, and one is a LOT more desirable than the other). Travel is a constant tug-of-war. You're pushed to take risks; you're pulled to play it safe. If we had to do it again, we'd have pushed ourselves more. But, we're thankful we pushed when we did!

37. Checking Things Off

Monday, August 30, 2004
Posted by Mike

Both of us are list people. We like—no, we MUST—make lists. It's our way of accomplishing things. Basically, if we could not make lists, we'd be two quivering bowls of jelly in the corner of life.

So, it's been a good day today, because we've checked off a few very important to-do items:

1. Goodbyes

First, we began to say goodbye to our kids in earnest. Heidi, brilliant woman that she is, had the idea of giving the kids each a pillowcase with their Kazakh name, their "new" name, and pictures ironed on the pillow. They are the same pictures we've been  showing them all along during our visits.

Heidi's mom gave us two blankets for the kids. Today, we talked to one caregiver for each child. We explained that we'd like to leave the pillowcase and blanket for the kids after we leave.

2. Trying to explain

Then, our translator explained to the kids that we would be coming back tomorrow, but then we had to leave for a while to go home and get things ready. Then, Momma and Apa (Grammie) would be coming back to get them.

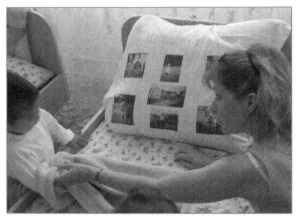

Well, it seemed like it went pretty well. Of course, our translator could have told them we would be busy plucking chickens next door for all we know. But it felt good to see the items on their beds and the blankets in their arms. We can leave knowing they will have remembrances of us until Heidi returns. (Isn't she a smart one?)

3. Date!

We SEEM to have a court date! We are indeed scheduled for 3:00 pm tomorrow (Tuesday). Now, as long as the judge returns from Almaty on time, we should be good to go. This, of course, is a big thing to check off.

4. And, we seem to have a court date. Did I mention that?

5. Trials and tribulations?

We met with our facilitator a few minutes ago and discussed the questions that may be asked by the judge tomorrow. By now we realize this IS a big deal. For example, there is a prosecutor. *A prosecutor?!* Great. Probably the Perry Mason of Taraz. We don't anticipate any potential disaster if we don't do a good job, but, clearly, this appears to be more than a "rubber stamp" for the adoption. I personally feel that, hey, we passed the "informal meeting" with the education committee, so we can do this, too.

However, the one thing people can't seem to understand is this: You have three kids. Why do you want to adopt MORE? Well, we say,

we've always wanted a large family. Then, why not just have more of your own? Well, we always wanted to complete our family through adoption. Why? Well, we say, we have been blessed in our lives with many things, and we want to share them with children who are orphaned and who  may never have a chance at a better life.

It is at this point that we are met with blank stares. Every time.

This seems to be a potential issue. There are also a few questions which will be given to us right before court. (!) Good luck preparing for that. The other thing is that, in order to reduce the chance of additional questioning, I am encouraged to address as many potential issues as possible in an opening statement. Sort of preemptively strike. Now, we were assured I would not be asked to make a speech. But clearly, I need to be practicing tonight on something that sounds an awful lot like a speech.

I'm not nervous. But I do feel like there is more responsibility on my shoulders tomorrow than I was led to believe...right up until this afternoon, when I was told otherwise. I know. Why should things be different now? :)

6. Food!
We also finally got a chance to eat at the famous Georgian restaurant everyone seems to talk about. It was actually open today. We ate outside in a beautiful shaded area. Heidi ordered a Georgian chicken specialty and I ordered lamb shashlik (like a kebab).

Well, we ended up getting TWO of each! In addition, we ordered this ridiculously good pancake (bread, really), with cheese, kind of baked/fried until it was crispy and chewy. Surprisingly, it was fat AND carb free. I heard the waiter say that, plain as day.

The awesome Georgian food. Juicy and crispy.

7. Pride.

Finally, we went to a mausoleum (another one) and a museum. We watched as the priest/shaman entered to begin singing the prayers. We also went to the Taraz museum. Both of us like museums, but both of us also instantly get tired the second we walk into any such door. But we enjoyed this one.

What sticks with me the most? A simple painting of three men.

They are the "founding fathers" of the three Hordes of Kazakhstan. Really. Kazakhstan started as three very large groups of nomadic people called hordes. I had read that every Kazakh can—and does—trace his or her heritage to one of the three hordes. I was a little skeptical about that. Do modern day young Kazakhs really still care about this? Is it embarrassing to them? Or maybe irrelevant?

So I asked our young interpreter, "Do you have any idea which horde you belong to?" He looked at me, puzzled, and said, "Of course." He then, with pride, explained that he was part of the Great Horde, and what the strengths of each of the groups were.

It left an impression on me. For some reason, looking at this simple, plain painting, at these proud men, helps me understand these people like nothing else has over this past month. I feel that I can look my two adopted children in the eye and tell them about their heritage now. And really believe it. I look forward to telling them when they get older.

The leaders of the three Hordes of Kazakhstan

So, it's Monday afternoon as I write. God willing, in 30 hours, we'll be on the night train to Almaty, and then, soon after, the plane back home. We are very excited about this. All day long, there is a "buzz" around all we do, knowing that, soon, we will be on our way home. To our (other) kids. Our goal for tonight is to prepare a bit for court, then give as little thought to tomorrow as we can.

Thankfully, the final hours of 24 season two are waiting!

Fun Documentary

The Eagle Huntress is a true story about a 13-year-old Kazakh girl who trains to become the first female in twelve generations to be an eagle huntress. Not hokey or hard to understand. Really informative and inspiring. Nik & Meg really liked it, even as teenagers!

HEIDI: I hoped the pillowcases and blankets would remind and reassure Nik and Meg of my return. They had several pictures of Mike and me, of Zack, Jake, and Brynn, of our house and of my parents, their new Grammie and Grampie. If they could look at their pillows during naps and as they went to bed each night, they would remember us and know I would return.

I was dreading court. I'm not a public speaker and I don't think quickly on my feet. To give a speech and answer impromptu questions, which I can't prepare for, was distressing.

It wasn't just fear of public speaking. I had wanted to adopt for so long, and I was hugely invested emotionally, making this situation even more intense. A final decision would be made that day in that courtroom. It was too much to take in. I prayed to God I wouldn't break down sobbing in court!

The Georgian restaurant was our most enjoyable meal in Taraz. We loved it. We loved it even more as it marked our last meal as we began wrapping up our time in Taraz.

The Good Life: Own

MIKE: The visit to the museum left such an impression on me, one I can recall clearly even now. These were proud people. They had been beaten down for so many years, but they never forgot their heritage and their identity. I've talked many times with Nik and Meg about what it means to be Kazakh. It's special.

We learned a lot from Ildos as we listened to the history of Kazakhstan. It seemed like he came to life when he told us of his heritage. He was very passionate about his country.

And we topped off our last day by finishing season two of *24*! Can't get better than that.

MIKE: The court date was looming. I felt nervous, but also quite confident that I could handle the speech well. I kept reminding myself, you're good at public speaking; at communicating to strangers. Remember, your job is to connect with these folks, just like you connect to other audiences. And, it was so exciting to be thinking we would be heading home.

We really had reached a milestone at this crossroads of Taraz.

The Good Life: Be & Plot
We had fought our way through the cultural and personal barriers enough to start viewing the people in a positive and respectful way. And we could actually see the future down the road with our children.

That last day had been one of the best days since we arrived in Kazakhstan. I'm so glad we had it. Because the next day would prove to be the hardest one of all.

Questions to consider
What examples do you see of Mike & Heidi moving "in the right direction?" What decisions have you made (or should make) to know you're going in the right direction for your Good Life?
*(Go to **NotFar.org/Kaz** for your free study guide.)*

155

Part 4

Breaking free

38. The Trial

Tuesday, August 31, 2004
Posted by Mike

In walked The Judge.

Slowly he moved to his desk and sat down. To our right, The Prosecutor and The Director (AKA, Imelda). To our left, two unnamed men..

I was standing. "Judge, you've gone too far," I said.

The judge stood up, spilling papers to the floor. "You are out of order!"

"No! You're out of order, sir!" I said. I turned to the prosecutor. "And you're out of order. You're ALL out of order!"

Nervously, the judge asked, "What's the truth, Mr. Vayda?"

"Truth?" I said incredulously. "Truth?!"

I paused and smiled grimly.

"You can't handle the truth!"

A huge murmur ran through the crowd. As I looked around, I saw that the people were saying, quite clearly, "Murmur!" The judge banged his gavel. "Order!" He yelled fruitlessly. "Ord—"

159

The door to the courtroom creaked open, and my Tom Cruise/Jack Nicholson/Al Pacino daydream was interrupted. A man walked in, said something in Kazakh, and everyone stood. Heidi and I did as well.

In walked The Judge.

We had been waiting for the trial to begin for over an hour. Thank God it wasn't too hot, because my suit jacket was stifling (just like the music room), and the tie I bought for this occasion was slowly closing my windpipe. The hour had gone very slowly. Imagine. We waited for over 60 minutes for this party to get  started. Sixty minutes of the heart beating fast, the prepared speech slowly running through the brain, the heart jumping as the door would open...and then close again.

By the time the judge actually walked in, I had pretty much lost my nervousness and was more than a little ticked off. In my mind, I had pictured him as the judge from *The Simpsons*. As it turns out, this judge was shorter and quite a bit more Kazakh than that. He looked up from his notes.

You want the truth? Here's the truth:
We had no idea how hard it was going to be to get these children.

Franz Kafka wrote a book called *The Trial*. It tells the story of a man who is brought before a judge and jury. But he never learns the charges. He is never told why he is in court or what the outcome will be. Each day in court is a day of absurdity, of questions that he cannot answer, of accusations he cannot defend against. When I read that book many years ago, I could never imagine I would be living something like it myself.

After some formalities, the judge invited me to speak. I stood and gave my opening speech. I was happy with the way I communicated. We had decided that we did not want to say anything that wasn't true. Even though there are a number of questions that we were encouraged to answer, shall we say, *creatively*, we crafted my speech to ignore those and instead answer very directly with honesty. We were encouraged to use my speech as a preemptive strike, addressing questions right up front. It seemed to work. He only asked a few questions. I answered them.

As I sat down, I have to admit, I thought, "Well, this should go pretty quickly now." It was clear in a few moments, however, that it was going to take as long as "he" wanted it to.

He asked Heidi to stand. He then proceeded to ask her the same questions that I had JUST answered a few minutes before! He asked her a number of questions, but the main sticking point seemed to be the fact that we already HAD three kids. If we wanted, he said through the interpreter, we could have more biologically. So why in the world would we want to adopt two unknown children? Did we try to adopt in the US? Did we try to adopt *American* children?

Over the next few minutes, it dawned on me (and that is a good way to describe it) that he was going to grill my unsuspecting wife. Of course, we were getting the questions—and answering the questions—through an interpreter, so who really knows what the exact questions were? And who really knows what our "answers" came out like on the other end?

If there was a defining moment, it was after a long series of questions to Heidi. I didn't know if she was really answering the way the judge wished. It just didn't seem like he was getting what he wanted. He sat back, looked away for a while, drumming his fingers on the desk.

I honestly thought, at that moment, *Wow. We could lose these kids.*

Then there was a four-way exchange between the judge, the two guys on the left, and the baby house director. It was a heated cacophony of Kazakh. Back and forth, back and forth.

As it went on, I thought, What if he said no? *What if he did?*

I actually began to get really indignant as I sat there waiting for him to continue. I formulated in my mind a response to him and his objections. I saw it very clearly. It was something like, "Look, sir. We have a stable home. We make more than enough money. I can guarantee you that we can give these children a life that is so much better than what they are faced with. Can you NOT see that what we have to offer is better than what they have now?"

I was ready to stop being quite so polite. I was getting tired of The Trial.

Then, quite suddenly, we were told to stand. We stood. We were told to leave. We left the room. As I watched the body language of the people, I realized. It would be okay. He called us back in briefly and said a bunch of words. Our translator—the man of few words—said, "Okay."

That was it. The judge wished us luck, told us the decision would be final in two weeks, and we walked out.

As we walked to the car, I ran through the whole trial in my head again. I can't go into details why, but we were led to believe that court would go smoothly, with little real stress. Not to mention, the other American couple had told us their trial went very easily.

Now, I've only been here a month. I don't know Kazakhs. I don't know what the normal adoption court is. Maybe it was all part of "the plan." Maybe it was business as usual today. But, like you, I've seen many courtroom dramas. And I think I have a sense of when the outcome has already been decided and it's just a matter of protocol to get to the ending everyone knows will occur.

But I'm being honest when I say, as far as this courtroom drama today, I really didn't know.

We will never know what the conversations were about in that room. Think about that. *We will never know.*

But you know what?

It does not matter now.

When we said goodbye to Nik and Meg tonight after court, we said goodbye to them as legally-approved parents.

Of course, we don't feel that way. We're both kinda dazed and confused.

But. We leave on the train to Almaty in a few hours. And we have accomplished every single thing we set out to three weeks ago, when we got off that same train at four am and were whisked to a waiting car.

In celebration/relief, we went to the hotel bar and bought two shots of Russian vodka. We toasted each other. *We did it.*

Thanks to all of you, our friends, for your prayers, your thoughts, your support. Although the true culmination of all of this will not occur until September 26, when Heidi comes off that plane with these children, today was the most important day.

This long, long trip is almost over.

We are so thankful you have traveled along the way with us.

HEIDI: Mike and I had several discussions before our day in court. How do we best respond, we wondered, in a way that makes sense to the Kazakh mind and culture, while also responding from our American perspective? This is actually much harder than you might think, especially when two little ones are at stake! Cultural barriers can be huge when attempting effective communication.

Mike did a great job in his opening statement (his notes are below). He answered all the questions right up front. I thought, phew, I'm off the hook. That fantasy was sure short lived! When it was my turn, the questions, my responses, the time standing became a never-ending blur.

My heart sank when the thought struck me during all the questioning that they are not going to let us have Nik and Meg.

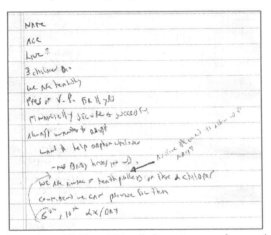

This conclusion came after repeatedly being asked the same question, over and over again. Why would I want to adopt when I already have three children? There didn't seem to be any comprehension to my responses. What else can I say?

Should I mention the miscarriages, and the heartbreak? Should I tell them I come from a large family that adopted internationally? As I'm wracking my brain, trying to find some way for the court to grasp why we wanted to adopt when we had three children, the questioning...stopped. I felt drained and emptied as we left the courtroom. I had no idea what the verdict would be. It was only when our interpreter said it was okay that I thought maybe I could believe him, maybe it would be all right. What a harrowing experience!

And just so you know...I did not break down sobbing!

MIKE: *As we sat in the hotel bar, (finally) having a Russian vodka, we went over all that happened. I'd worked so hard on that speech. Although I've made a career in communications, it was the most nervous I've ever been. Imagine my shock when I realized that my* *quiet wife was the one who would be grilled instead of me. My shock quickly turned to anger. This was not what they told us to prepare for. Why didn't they warn us? Why didn't they help us expect this kind of inquisition? And now we were at their mercy, unprepared. When the questioning finally ended, I was furious, not relieved.*

After she sat down, I grabbed Heidi's hand. I have never been more proud of her.

Time and time again during this trip, we experienced a feeling of complete powerlessness. And now, here we were, in a foreign country, in a courtroom with unknown laws, unable to understand or communicate,

utterly dependent on what our translator said...and the judge. We had no legal representation (Maybe we should have? But if so, why didn't someone suggest it?) Everything we had been prepped for...did not happen. We were blindsided. And we were alone.

As I said in the blog, we'll never know what that heated conversation was about that suddenly ended the trial. I do know God is called a friend to the fatherless; that He gives a name to the nameless. I will never be able to explain why, of course, but I believe we had help that day in the courtroom.

God brought a father and a mother to two little orphaned Kazakhs. And we named them Nik and Meg.

39. A Whirlwind Followed by Waiting

Wednesday, September 1, 2004
Posted by Heidi

After court we said goodbye to our new American friends. We gave them all the items we no longer needed—including 24 Season 1, which we will miss almost as much as the kids (that was Mike talking, and you know he's joking!).

We said goodbye to Meg and Nik (and our friend, the director! As you can see, she was very happy for us).

We called home and gave them the news, news we were still trying to accept ourselves. We then packed up, getting ready for the overnight train. We left the hotel at 10 pm to catch the train at 11 pm. We slept pretty well in our four-bed cabin (our facilitator was with us). For a while there Mike and I wondered if the director of the baby house might also be bunking with us to Almaty but, alas, she did not.

We arrived in Almaty at 9 am today and were driven to an apartment. We were told we would have a meeting this afternoon. We went for a walk and, after many, many blocks and a bit of a search, we found the café we went to when we were here before. It seemed a lifetime ago when we were there last. And was that cappuccino good!

Not from the Hotel Zhambyl!

Almaty definitely feels like a metropolitan city after being in Taraz for three weeks. We found our way back to the apartment and have just been waiting for this meeting to take place.

Our flight leaves at 4 am so we'll leave the apartment around 1 am. So far all has gone smoothly, and we are very grateful! After how busy we've been, it seems strange to be waiting. We look forward to getting on that plane and heading home!

Galina, our facilitator

HEIDI: While wrapping up our last-minute errands and saying our last goodbyes, I gradually began to feel the adoption of these two children was in fact going to happen. It seemed that all was actually going to be okay. What a relief for court to be behind us. Saying goodbye to Nik and Meg was bittersweet, even though they did seem to take it well.

Curly Surprise

Before leaving the baby home, I was asked if I wanted Nik and Meg's hair cut. Their hair was already very short so I declined the offer. Keeping the children's hair short is for ease of care and minimizing bug issues, I'm sure. I had an inkling that Meg might have curly hair. My hunch turned out to be correct. Meg has beautiful curly black hair!

Sleeping with strangers (on trains that is) is not unusual, but sleeping with Galina was. If you recall, on our way to Taraz, after depositing us in our own cabin, she promptly disappeared. Nonetheless, we arrived in Almaty the next morning none the worse for wear.

The apartment was a place to rest and relax until our late night flight.

The meeting we were scheduled for was brief and uneventful. No complaints there!

MIKE: *I honestly have no memory of our time back in Almaty, or sleeping with two women on the train. I guess I was too scarred from the trial. Reading the blog again does bring back a memory of that long, long walk to glorious cappuccino. A gift from heaven, to be sure.*

The Good Life: Plot

Heidi said it felt like a lifetime since we were at that café'. In a sense, it was. We were living a different life now. We were different people. Parents of five! A multicultural family! Things would never be the same.
We were just beginning to plan a new future.

40. Thank God Almighty, Free at Last!

Friday, September 3, 2004
Posted by Mike

Our Thursday began at 1:15 am, when we were picked up at the apartment in Almaty to catch our flight. Our Thursday ended 34 hours later, when we crawled into our king-sized bed in Buckfield, Maine with our (other) children. Cancelled flights, unplanned bus trips, and jet lag aside, the trip home was fine.

As I sit here, fuzzy brained, surfing the web at ludicrous speed (so fast, it makes a grown man cry!), I am very thankful we are home.

Although we don't even want to think about it yet, Heidi is leaving in a little over a week. And, after being gone for a month, there is mail to wade through, bills to pay, Tivo'd shows to watch. And don't even THINK of telling us who won *The Amazing Race*. (We've kinda been on our own.)

Jake and I went out to get some milk this morning. As I drove my car for the first time in 30+ days, I looked around and realized that summer is gone. Fall is here. Zack is in school today. Our three kids looked so big to us last night when we hugged them. Time moves on.

I looked over at my son Jake, seeing him smiling up at me. I am thanking God for safety, for health, for bringing us back home again.

We'll be enjoying this weekend. So much.

— NOW —

HEIDI: Home, home at last! Seeing our kids was beyond description! Driving up our driveway in the dark, walking into our home, hugging and talking to our kids all felt strangely and wonderfully familiar. As exhaustion soon set in, we found our way to bed. It was no longer the twin beds of the Zhambyl Hotel in Taraz. It was our own bed, which easily made way for three very brave, strong, special kids.

MIKE: Adventures are nice but, sometimes, boring can be bliss. The trip back home, even though it was halfway across the world and had some delays and annoyances, really was uneventful. Almost before we knew it, we were back in the USA again.

Our house seemed gargantuan to me; my kids seemed older and bigger (which made me a little sad, thinking what I had missed forever in exchange for our adoption), and my bed seemed like the lap of luxury. Every moment together was a gift.

Best Parts of Being Home

1. The kids! Seeing our three children
2. The peace and quiet of rural Maine
3. The width and length of a California king-sized bed
4. Everything in English
5. Driving again!
6. Drinking water from the tap
7. Long showers
8. A kitchen—our own food!
9. TV shows
10. Always-on internet (no dialing and waiting)

41. Silence Rarely Sounded so Good

Saturday, September 4, 2004
Posted by Mike

It's 7:45 am, and I've been up since five. Welcome to "reverse jet lag." Everyone else, including Heidi, is still sleeping, so I'm taking advantage of the time to get caught up on my email as well as a quick post here.

Before I got up, I laid in bed and listened to how absolutely quiet it was. Even now, only the crickets are making any noise. What a contrast to downtown Taraz! Living in the country may have its issues but, man, is this silence golden. It made me glad all over again for the choice we made to live here.

Our first day back home yesterday proved to be anything but peaceful. We realized that we needed to get the visa process going ASAP if we were to get them in time for Heidi's next trip. With the holiday weekend (Labor Day), the forms, money orders, passports, and photos needed to be Fedexed by end of day yesterday. So, even though it was very painful, we took a breath and jumped right back into the paperwork again. Took us most of the morning to get it all ready. The rest of the day was spent going through mail, finances, and shuffling around the big house in a daze. Both of us kept thinking, *We're actually here.*

We did manage, however, to finish our day well. We had our nachos.

Did you hear?

We had our nachos. Heidi made her awesome guacamole, and all five of us crowded onto the couch to begin getting caught up on *Amazing Race.* I remember well the FOUR Fridays away from our kids and our home and our nachos. It was very hard. Which made last night all the more wonderful.

Today we hope to restart some sort of routine. As crazy as it is, routine will help all of us find peace amidst our joy. There are bills to pay, a lawn to mow, a house to clean...but then again, it is a holiday weekend, right? Maybe we'll ease into this a little more slowly.

Sad to say, but Heidi leaves a week from Monday again. The best mindset seems to be to just keep truckin' until this is all finally finished and *everyone* is home. So, we're in a small respite right now, before the next chaos.

Still though, both of us are so thankful to be here, now.

HEIDI: It was a sad realization in my blurry, jet-lagged state that downtime was not an option. For my sake and for the sakes of those around me, I had to accept that my time home needed to be about "the list." I just wanted to hang out with the kids, especially knowing I would be gone again in a matter of days. Instead, I had to be grateful for the small pockets of time with them. I kept telling myself how we'll have all the time in the world, in just a few weeks.

The entire visa application and packet for myself and for my mother had to be completed and Fedexed that day, which even then would be an unusually quick turnaround time for approval. I'm not really sure how we managed getting the application and all the other documents out that would allow us to travel, but we somehow got it done. Labor Day left us with just five business days to get our paperwork back. It was pretty stressful but we kept our fingers crossed.

A Lifelong Love Affair

To this day, every time one of our kids comes home, they request Heidi's nachos. Amazing how powerful food is when it comes to feeling loved.

MIKE: Even during all the flurry of work and the joy of being with our kids, in the back of my mind I was thinking about Heidi leaving again. To be honest, I was really worried about being the only parent to my kids. At that stage of our lives, I was on the road a great deal, and Heidi was the primary caregiver. So the thought of taking on that role—with Heidi all the way over in Kazakhstan!—was worrisome. Even though it was so good to be home, I was already feeling impending dread.

42. Eyes on the Prize

Thursday, September 9, 2004
Posted by Mike

It's been a week since we've come home.

Actually, at this time last week, we were somewhere over the Atlantic. Maybe we were still in Frankfurt. Point is, I find it difficult to believe we've already been home almost a week.

It's been weird being back, to be honest with you. I've got a couple observations for you this morning. They may be random, but they all have one thing in common: What's going through our minds, post-Trip One, and pre-Trip Two:

1. **Truly amazing how quickly you get used to life as you knew it.** When we were in Kaz, we longed to be home. We ached for the familiar. Now that we're back, it's like we were never away! All those things you swear never to take for granted? They so easily become part of the wallpaper again. And in such a short time, too. The embarrassment of riches we have in our supermarkets, the fact that driving is still a relatively non-contact sport, dozens of Tivo'd shows to watch whenever I choose, blisteringly fast, always-on internet, nachos at my beck and call...I find it a mystery how one can retain "lessons learned" when so much is here, so easily. So constantly.

2. In a few days, I'm Mr. Mom.

Maybe the fact that I'll be the only parent in a home that desperately needs two will help with point #1, huh? I gotta tell ya, I am in no way looking forward to Heidi going back. Oh sure, she's got a tough job ahead of her. She's heading back to Kaz in all its glory. She (and her mom) have to travel, deal with a different language, get these two kids home. But, has anyone thought about the fact that I have to, like, *cook*?

Right now, the thought of two weeks without Heidi is pretty discouraging. But it's clear that I've let my guard down, so to speak, in this week. We both had the right mindset while we were gone: You deal with what you have right in front of you, period. You take it one step at a time. You tell yourself you CAN do this. And you remind yourself at all times, like Igor said in *Young Frankenstein*, it could be worse. It could always be worse. It's time for that mindset.

3. Miles still to go before we sleep.

We (okay, I) need to regroup. Take a deep breath, and understand we still have a lot to do to bring these kids home.

4. Eyes on the prize.

That phrase kept popping into my head while we were gone. Get through the problems right in front of you by looking fixedly at the goal. This has not changed.

Now, I certainly do not intend to compare the hardships of the civil rights struggle to our current challenges. However, people through the centuries have overcome difficulties of all kinds by remembering this promise of the ultimate triumph of Good.

In a sense, we are joining with them in a fight for justice. Our goal, our hope, is the same. We are fighting against distance, cultures, bureaucracy, loneliness, finances, fears, and our own weaknesses to bring two children out of poverty and into our family.

We are going to make a difference. The Prize is clear, and not that far away.

5. Baby steps to the plane. Baby steps to the kitchen to cook.

Heidi leaves on Monday. As we regroup (reload?) for this final push, it really is one step at a time.

I take great comfort in the support that you will be giving Heidi with your thoughts and prayers for her and her mom.

And me? I have a microwave. We take miracles where we get 'em.

HEIDI: It is surprising how quickly we assimilated back into life as we knew it.

Can you sense Mike's anxiety? Mike has travelled all over the world for business. That's familiar territory for him. Home alone? Not so much. I'm used to being home or, if I'm traveling, it is with Mike. Our roles were reversed in this situation, causing trepidation and uncertainty for both of us. We reminded ourselves again and again to take one step at a time, "baby steps" (*What About Bob...again!*).

MIKE: Yeah. I was a nervous wreck. Even as Heidi and I are writing this, she is laughing at my post. I know I sound overly dramatic!

Usually in life, what we worry about isn't nearly as bad as when it actually happens. I kept telling myself that. But I had a hard time believing it.

The Good Life: Plot

"Eyes on the prize." We needed to remember the plot of our new life. We had accomplished so much! We fought through The Trial; we arrived back home; reconnected with Zack, Jake, and Brynn; successfully finished the paperwork to get Heidi and Barbara legal for the trip back.
But, to me, it felt like a big step backward to have them leave.
There was still so much more to do and to learn on this journey.
It was going to be a new challenge: being apart from each other,
so we could all be together. We needed to stick to the plot.

Throughout the book, we've highlighted times when we discovered what we call the Seven Elements to the Good Life. This next leg of our journey, when we were apart, playing different roles, was the time we really began to picture the life we never knew we wanted, and how to live it.

Questions to consider

*In "Breaking free," Mike & Heidi faced opposition to bring Nik & Meg home. What are some examples? What opposition have you faced when trying to get closer to your Good Life? How did it affect you?
(For more questions and your **free** study guide,
go to **NotFar.org/Kaz***

Part 5

Off you go...again

43. I Like it Better when I Leave

Tuesday, September 14, 2004
Posted by Mike

Although I haven't heard from her, Heidi (and Barbara, her mom) should have touched down in Almaty a little while ago.

We took a picture with Roland (her dad) and Barbara before we left for the airport. As we said goodbye yesterday, I realized how it must feel for Heidi when I leave for business trips. I can tell you, without hesitation, it's better to be the one leaving than the one staying.

The folks at the USAir counter were obviously bumming due to the bankruptcy announcement earlier that day. The picture of us with Nik and Meg seemed to break the tension in the air and give them something else to think about. There were several "Awwwws" and, "Let me see!" but, although they really tried, they couldn't find any options to get them home any earlier. So, we resigned ourselves to two weeks apart and let it go. As I walked out, they all asked me to bring the kids by to see them.

Our first day at home without Mom was okay. Dad is trying to learn how to get his work done while taking care of the kids at the same time. Thankfully, there are no pressing projects going on right now. We went for a walk in the woods yesterday afternoon. It was a beautiful fall day (as is today), and I wanted to enjoy it. We had a good walk, but Zack was struggling a bit being without Mom. Overall, we enjoyed the great day, even though it felt very different.

Probably the biggest news of the day yesterday was that I, Mike, cooked hamburger.

What else is there to say? I mean, I. Cooked. Hamburger.

There were no smoke alarms going off. There were no flash fires.

Next up? Soufflé!

Well. Hopefully, we'll have news from Heidi tomorrow. As you can see, there's not much inspiration flowing from this keyboard today!

— NOW —

HEIDI: Here I am leaving my family...again, in order to get the rest of my family! I was glad to have my mother with me for the second part of this adventure. Mom raised thirteen children, so she knows kids. She's also traveled internationally. One Mom trip is worth telling you about.

When I was about 11, Mom traveled to Thailand, intending to adopt two infants. She expected to be gone three weeks but, instead, it was nearly three months! And, on her flight back with two three-month-old babies, she missed her connecting flight in Paris. She was all alone for a night in some hotel, with little money and limited formula and diapers for the babies before she was able to get the next available flight. Oh, and she was also *pregnant*, by the way.

Meanwhile, in Maine, our whole family drove three hours to Boston where my mother, who had been gone for so long, did NOT get off the plane. We were devastated and incredibly worried. Back then there were no cell phones and no texting. It wasn't until we returned back home that, somehow, Mom got through to Dad. What a relief for everyone when Mom and David and Mindy, our new baby brother and sister, finally arrived.

How's that for an extraordinary story?! Now back to ours.

It would've been nice for all of us to get back to the US sooner, but the earliest available flights we could book using miles meant staying in Almaty a few extra days.

I never felt certain that this adoption was a sure thing. Not UNTIL we were ALL safely home in the US. Even though many hurdles had been jumped and so much had already been accomplished and we were so close to the end, it still was not The End.

MIKE: *My father-in-law Roland and I took Heidi and Barbara to the airport in Portland. The kids were with us. That trip back home was so* *quiet! You had two men who were both on the verge of panic, realizing their beloveds were gone.*

It wasn't all selfish thoughts. I was really, really worried about Heidi traveling without me. Of course she's tough and she's a world traveler, but any husband can relate, I'm sure: She was going to a country halfway around the world and, if anything happened, I could not help her in any way, shape, or form.

We stopped to buy some flowers on the way home; some mums (because ours was missing. Get it?). The colors of fall were beautiful, but all of us were feeling very alone and blue.

The Good Life: Clarify

Writing this, I just realized: Zack, Jake, and Brynn were without their mother for a very long time. Not just the first trip, but a *second* trip, as well, with only a hectic week between to spend with her. These are the unspoken costs of foreign adoption. I know a lot of children have it far worse. But I also know all that time without their mother must have been so hard. When I say the adoption was a whole family mission, this is what I mean. It helped us clarify what was really important in life.

44. Waiting Game

Wednesday, 15, September 2004
Posted by Mike

I FINALLY got a call from my gallivanting, globe-trotting wife last night. (Not that it bothered ME that she didn't call earlier, you understand. I was just, um, concerned for the kids.)

They had arrived in Taraz a few hours earlier at 4 am, and, after a brief nap, were ready to start the all-important day.

They have (had, by now) a busy day. She said she would try to call this morning before they were leaving from Taraz back to Almaty with the kids.

What a crazy time! Flying to Kaz, then a train to Taraz, then back to Almaty, almost without stopping.

With the kids. Can you believe it? If all has gone well, she will HAVE the kids in her possession, even now.

Something good (and pretty wild) to think about. I'll keep you posted as I hear more.

HEIDI: I know firsthand the waiting game. I often wondered what was happening and how things were progressing when Mike was away on his business trips. I am sure the waiting and wondering was even harder for Mike with so much riding on this particular trip.

The Good Life: Be

MIKE: More "adoption costs": the worry and nervousness, waiting to hear if my wife was safe. That silence, from the time we said goodbye at the airport, until she called, was a long, lonely, scary quiet. I gained a whole new appreciation for Heidi and her role as mom and master of the home.

I also found out I was a lot more of a worrier than I ever thought. (Heidi just chuckled and said sarcastically, "Oh really?")

You just don't think of these things when you're on the road like I was. At that time of my career, I was producing conferences in the US and in Europe, and my mind was always taken up with the job. Now, I was home, with plenty of time to conjure up all kinds of "what if's."

It did help me with some control issues. I simply had to have faith. It was all I could do.

45. Into Kaz, Out of Taraz!

Friday, September 17, 2004
Posted by Heidi

I just received this from Heidi...they seem to be doing fine, but tired.

Here's a recap of our trip so far:

Our flight to Frankfurt was fine. Then, a loooong five-hour wait for the next plane. When we arrived in Kaz, Mom and I got a good night's sleep in our new home away from home in our Almaty apartment. On this day we went for a walk before getting food items for the apartment and spent a long time finding the right store to buy two umbrella strollers. There was a short time to repack before leaving to meet our facilitator for the overnight train to Taraz.

At 4 am, Mom and I arrive in Taraz and are driven to the hotel to get a few more hours' sleep. At 11 am we go to a registration office for Meg and Nik's birth certificates. And now, two weeks after leaving Meg and Nik, I am going to see them again! How will they react after being away from them this long? How will they react to Grammie (Apah)?

We were sent to a room and the kids were brought to us. It was so good to see them again! They both gave me a hug and, after only a minute, Nik was over to see Apah. Apah has a cool camera case with two zippers! This kept Nik busy and curious for the hour we were with them. Meg, the girl I know and love, wanted me to hold her and that's what I did. Meg, though, kept eyeing Apah to see what she was all about. I explained to Meg and Nik at the end of our visit that I would be back that night to get them and we would ride the train.

After seeing the kids, one of our American friends arranged for Mom and me to see an older children's orphanage. We enjoyed and appreciated the chance to take this tour. Mom took several pictures, which the children there seemed to like.

Mom and I ate at a restaurant I had been to on the first trip and then we collapsed for a few hours. We were exhausted! After making a call home we packed again for the overnight train. This time, though, I was packing clothes for Meg and Nik, too.

At 9 pm we went to the baby home. Meg was woken from sleep to get on her new clothes and shoes. Then we went to Nik's group. The kids were still awake and were excited to see us. They may have been kept up to see us and to say "sowbol" (goodbye) to Nik. I changed him into his new clothes and shoes, said our goodbyes and were off.

It was hard to see some of the caregivers saying goodbye, knowing how much they cared for Meg and Nik. You could tell it was emotional for some of them.

To the train we went. How would this go? Quite well, I have to say! Nik cried a few times through the night. The problem was he was thirsty. That taken care of, they both slept well (it was somewhat cramped, though, with Meg, Nik, and me in one train bed!) They were interested in the train and were not fearful at all.

But there is something even more interesting about this train trip. Some of you may remember Mike joking about maybe the baby home director would be sleeping with us on the train. Well, it was not the baby home director on this overnight train. Who was it, you ask? It was the judge's wife! I am not kidding! We had six in a four-berth cabin and the judge's wife to top it off!

Yes, indeed, this has been quite a ride!

We returned to our "home" in Almaty at 9 am today. It will be nice to get to know Meg and Nik more over the next week before returning to the states. They both had a long nap this afternoon. Momma, too.

What a week!

HEIDI: We stayed just about a week in our Almaty apartment. I hoped that, by getting it situated beforehand with food and supplies, it would make it easier when the four of us returned from Taraz.

After arriving, our errands and a well-deserved nap, Mom and I packed what we needed for ourselves and for Nik and Meg for this quick trip to Taraz. Being disoriented by jet lag and the time difference seemed of little consequence compared to the full ONE day getting Nik and Meg we anticipated.

There was so much happening in such a short time. We slept when we could and looked only at the next thing in front of us. The number of times I packed and repacked over these two months was crazy. To keep track of what we'd need for where and for who and for how long was a mind-boggling feat in itself.

Top Packing Tips

1. Make a list.
2. Always keep essentials with you (passport, paperwork, ID, money, etc.).
3. Check the list repeatedly.
4. Get great joy as you cross out items!
5. Consider a money belt, even if they are dorky.

I was unsure how Nik and Meg would respond after our separation but they seemed to remember me and were happy to see me. I was pleased how Nik immediately took to Mom. Meg was guarded, of course. but she did not act scared or upset during our short visit.

I knew that, if there was one place Mom would want to visit, it would be an orphanage. She has a huge heart for children! As I've mentioned previously, my parents adopted five children from around the world, which makes thirteen children altogether. Wherever she goes she is wondering how she can make a difference in a child's life.

What a surreal evening. Mom and I were driven by night from the hotel to the baby home where we clothed two children and whisked them away. Considering how foreign this was for Nik and Meg, they seemed fairly unfazed. Saying goodbye forever to the only world they've ever known is probably not a concept three years olds grasp.

We piled in the car and were well on our way to the train station when Mom realized I did not have the pillowcases or blankets I'd given Nik and Meg. The driver quickly took us back. I fretted we'd miss the train when the search for these items took so long. With two pillowcases and only one blanket, I rushed back to the car. We made it to the train station just in time.

Sadly, my guess is Nik and Meg did not have their pillowcases and blankets after Mike and I left. It was not a good sign if they didn't even know where they were. Also, clothing and items are for everyone in the baby home. Mike and I saw this ourselves when we'd spot the same clothes on different children from day to day.

Nik, Meg, and I slept on one narrow train bunk. Keeping Nik and Meg as quiet as possible took some doing. No pressure, either, with Galina AND the judge's wife bunking with us!

I was happy, relieved, and tired when the FOUR of us finally arrived at our Almaty apartment.

The Good Life: Power & Presence

MIKE: As you read these posts, you'll see Heidi discovering and living the Elements of *Power* and *Presence*. She is absolutely awesome at planning, organizing, and facilitating. And she turns generic spaces into home, wherever we go. Throughout this section of the journey, you will see her at her strongest. She is in a foreign country, with two newly-adopted children, not even knowing the language...and she *kills* it. She makes it all *work*. She finds new habits and routines (Power) to make things feel as normal as possible in a crazy atmosphere. And then she focuses on her built-in strengths and abilities to succeed. This is Presence: Confidently thriving in your uniqueness; the true Good Life. It's what we all long for; this is what it looks like. Man, am I proud of her.

46. A Missed Opportunity

Saturday, September 18, 2004
Posted by Mike

You may recall "The Trial" we had, and how challenging it was for us. So how weird is it that Heidi is sharing a small cramped train berth with the wife of the JUDGE?! For a ten hour trip!

I sure wish she would've taken advantage of the opportunity to grill HER! I can see it now:

"So, Mrs. Judge's Wife—IF that is your real name—you're on a train from Taraz to Almaty. Tell the court, please, why do you want to go to ANOTHER city when you already LIVE in a city?! Why isn't having one city of your OWN enough? Why do you find the need to want MORE cities??"

Oh, that would've been rich.

Kidding! I'm kidding.

No news from Heidi today. It's been awesome to be home with Zack and Jake and Brynn. The fall is settling in. I spent most of my time answering emails and taking care of the kids. When I stop to think that two more kids will be coming home soon, I have a hard time getting my head around that. Crazy!

— NOW —

MIKE: *Seems I got a little cocky in that post! I was in the US, and I guess I forgot who might be reading.*

For the upcoming posts when Heidi is in Kaz, you can just picture me in Maine with the three older kids. There's not much for me to add! I missed my wife; I worried for her safety; I played a new role of caregiver; I gained weight eating snack foods and watching TV during the long lonely nights.

The biggest stress for me was trying to do my work at the same time. I did find it was difficult to settle back into my job again. So much had happened! Trying to pick up where I left off was very hard to do. Life was so different; how could work be the same?

It was hard, but nothing compared to my wife and her challenges.

And there you have my life for the next several posts!

47. Snak-ey Business

Posted by Heidi
Saturday, September 18, 2004

Yesterday afternoon we went to the office of "The Sisters." This time it was for Meg and Nik's passports and visas. The women at the office tried to take Meg but...no way! She stayed right with Momma. After a while Nik went with the women and did fine. He was given an apple and that really helped (although I did ask them to keep an eye on him while he was eating that thing!). After two hours of writing and signing papers, I was done.

It was 7 pm when we left so we went to the Ramstore (the mini mall) and ate supper. I spent the rest of the evening trying to finish writing and sending the post to Mike. No small task. It was 11 pm when I got Meg and Nik to bed.

Now, in case you didn't know, this apartment is a very exciting place! If you've ever had a toddler, you know what I mean. Magnetized glass doors, light switches, locks, and even ripping paper into small pieces is great fun! As I write, the living room light is going on and off. Trying to maneuver a dark bathroom is not easy, either!

 Maybe you can guess which one of these two kids I am speaking of. Then again, how could I be in the bathroom alone? As soon as I am

191

out of Meg's sight, she wails. Needless to say, there were three of us in the bathroom while I showered and got ready this morning. Memories of the toddler years are flooding back.

A girl from the office offered to accompany us to an amusement park today. This was a big help. We walked around, mostly observing. There were a few kiddie rides. She asked if they wanted to ride but both said no. She helped us order lunch. A group of children were having a birthday party. Part of the entertainment included a man pulling two huge snakes out of a box!

Just when I thought the show was over, the man pulled out an even bigger snake! (That's the picture here.)

Well, with the third snake put back in the box, we are ready to pay our bill. No, wait...the show is not over! The hugest snake I've ever seen is pulled out! This thing is wrapped around the guy's neck and all the kids are oohing and aahing (with some screaming, too, but I won't say from whom).

Wow, what a lunch!

Nik had this look of concern the whole time we were out, whether it was about snakes, food, or rides. Meg seemed to notice some pictures and other children but, besides that, I think the new sights and sounds are just a lot to take in. We returned "home." Little doses at a time. Baby steps!

Nap time. For Meg, anyway. Nik is not so eager. After a crying spell he dropped off to sleep...and...15 minutes later woke up. Meg awoke at that point. So much for nap time. Nik has been fussy since getting up. Mom and I are trying to figure out the possible reasons. Time will work these things out.

HEIDI: Imagine how overwhelming everything was for Nik and Meg! They'd probably never been out of the baby home until Mike and I came along. Even the office visit was a lot for them.

I remember that evening as I considered the office visit and our day at the park and realized Nik and Meg were probably more in shock than anything else. New people and new places at every turn had to be traumatic.

The Good Life: Clarify
I decided I should not overdo it with too many activities. Instead, focus on what is most important. I find this is always the best strategy when things get crazy: only do what you must do, and do it well.

The apartment was virtually an amusement park, anyway. Who needs more?

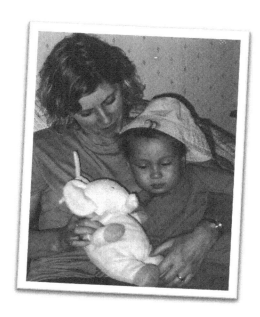

48. Election Day
& the Supermarket Adventure

Posted by Heidi
Sunday, September 19, 2004

(Here's Heidi's next post. Call me crazy, but things seem a bit less exotic here in Buckfield.

I talked to her this morning, and I asked her to rate how she's really doing. She said an "8." Of course, she's so tough, she'd probably say that if her leg was being gnawed by ferrets.

I'm very proud of her. She's doing a phenomenal job. And the fact that she is actually sending pictures and posts in addition to all the adjustments going on over there too?! As we say in Maine, she's a keepah.)

First of all, Mom and I now know why Nik was fussy. He pooped in the potty chair two times and was then a different boy. New foods and schedules do that to a person. Meg does not mind using her pull-ups as her bathroom. The problem is, I could not find pull-ups small enough for her. Consequently, she has gone through several pull-ups and pants.

Today is election day. Who is being elected? The deputies. I am not sure who that is, but we were told it might be better not to be on the roads today. We stuck to the sidewalks. After spending a lot of time looking at a map to recognize the name of our street and a few others, we decided to be adventurous and look for a supermarket. I wanted to find some of the foods Mike and I have eaten in restaurants but be able to take it "home." The first milestone was to actually see the letters and recognize those same letters on the side of the building. Great, the right street. Now which direction? Downhill here is north, which really throws me off, but I know that so we head...mmm...downhill.

Mom and I are trying to have Meg and Nik in the strollers for the first time to see how they do. We take the kids in and out several times because of stairs along the way. Not too easy. After five blocks I am looking to the right for the market. It must be here but it sure does look more like a casino than a grocery store!

Inside, first we have to check our bags, which is a pain. I took out my money and passport and left the rest. I find some Pampers. They are not pull-ups but they are smaller. I ordered four or five food items at a counter, then paid at the cashier aisle. I even got my bag back on the way out!

There were booths with ready-to-eat foods and tables nearby to sit. I got two doner kebabs in a tortilla wrap, an Uzbeki bread, plov (rice) and a "cheeseburger." We sat down to eat.

A guy that appeared to be overseeing our set of tables came up and said something. I said "English?" and he responded with "humph" and walked away. Since I was now not sure it was okay to eat there, we quickly finished. It was a nice walk back with a park running alongside us part of the way. It was quite a hike but worth the sense of satisfaction having located the market. Meg and Nik did great in their strollers for the first time and we have supper for tonight!

Meg is laying down and is ready for her nap. Nik has been crying for fifteen minutes or so. I am thinking he does not settle down easily. He has gone to the bathroom and has eaten so he seems mostly upset that he has no toys and has to lay down. This is reminding me of Jake. He did not settle easily, no matter how tired he was.

Nik's just like you, Jake!

HEIDI: I do like trying to figure things out. Why not get outside and attempt a walk to the market? It was a challenge to follow a Russian/Kazakh map with Russian/Kazakh street names. It took longer than expected but mission accomplished. We did it!

It was pivotal that Nik and Meg get used to the strollers since Mom and I would be relying on them heavily in airports during our extensive trip home.

Were Nik and Meg hungry, tired, scared, sad? With the language barrier it was hard to know.

Mike asked recently, "Do you remember feeling scared being there?" Actually, overall, the people were quite welcoming and friendly. And the experiences I had, I have been able to share with Nik and Meg.

The Good Life: Amplify
It would have been easy to play it safe, hunkering down in the apartment until it was time to fly home. Would two white women with two Kazakh children stand out? Possibly. But I knew I would regret not taking advantage of this opportunity to get out and see Nik and Meg's country of birth. Fortunately, there were no incidents.

49. Movies, Physicals & Gummy Bears!

Monday, September 20, 2004
Post by Barbara (or, as Nik says, "Gammie")

(This is Mike. We've passed the less-than-one-week-left mark. They'll all be back next Sunday night. Here in Maine, the kids are still speaking to me, so I guess the Vayda Family is surviving this so far. Now on to Barbara.)

A few evenings ago, Heidi and I decided to use my laptop to show the kids a "Baby Einstein" DVD. But, alas, after 20 minutes the picture disappeared. When we finally got it started again, we had to start at the beginning again. Then this same thing began happening about every five minutes. So much for "TV night!"

Later, via phone, Mike walked Heidi through the process of straightening out our dilemma. So, last night we tried again, showing the kids a Sesame Street DVD. Great! It works well! The kids watched the whole thing.

Learning about Nik
Nik has been having a hard time at nap time, crying, not wanting to go to sleep, then again afterwards for some unknown reason. Yesterday after the nap, he cried and cried, stopping only when offered a light snack, then continued crying longer. In our efforts to

figure this out, we decided that today, after nap time, we would offer him a meal to see if this makes a difference.

Back to movie time. Since Nik has a hard time going to bed, last night we decided to try letting him stay up and see how long he'd last before going to sleep on his own. So, after the kids watched a movie, Heidi and I put one in for ourselves. Soon Nik was off to play. We underestimated him, for at midnight he was still playing!! I think he would have outlasted us...had we not decided it WAS bedtime for him, too. I think he'd make a great candidate for the "Survivor" series with his abilities to out-last, out-wit, and out-play! Of course, Meg had fallen asleep in Heidi's arms. Getting to know the kids takes lots of experimenting, but it's a fun challenge.

Physicals
Today was the appointment for the kids' physicals. This is really a very basic checkup without shots or anything painful. Nik weighed 22 lbs. and was 32.6 inches tall. Meg was 17.6 lbs. and was 31.6 inches tall. While there, the doctor wanted to see their throats, so in turn he gave each of them, starting with Nik, a Gummy Bear. Nik didn't want to put that in his mouth! It went in once between nearly sealed lips and came right back out. We tried more, but he wouldn't keep it in his mouth, and I don't know if the doctor got to see his throat or not.

Now, Meg, on the other hand, popped hers right in and ate it. Mmmm...good! After we left the doctor's room, then I put the Gummy Bear in Nik's mouth once more. I think he'd licked it enough so that now he was tasting it and this time he ate it! Sooooo many new experiences for them.

About me
This is a wonderful experience for me, too. In Taraz, when we went to the baby home, Nik's group was still up (at 9 pm). I hadn't seen them before, so I managed to get one picture of some of them. Then they decided to play games on me. I'd hold up my camera for another picture and they'd laugh and run away. I also shook hands with a few of the braver ones. What cute kids! I was having a blast with them! But, I couldn't help wondering...how many of them will find a forever family as Nik and Meg have? How many of them will grow up in orphanages and never have the loving stability of their own family? My heart aches for them!

Probably 20 minutes after leaving the baby home, we realized we had forgotten the important pillowcases and blankets that had been left for the kids. The driver (to our great joy) turned around and back we went. Fortunately, we'd planned for extra time. Heidi left the car to go in with our facilitator and managed to fetch both pillowcases and one blanket. While they were gone, Nik started pointing to his new sandals, new socks, new pants, and a new shirt. He was impressed, I'm sure!

The kids were so good on the train, too. It was interesting to watch their expressions when they woke the next morning. Nik opened his eyes and saw Heidi first thing. Heidi smiled at him and he smiled back; it was like saying, "I'm glad to be with you today instead of at the baby home." Meg also smiled as she awoke on the train. A great start for the first day!

Learning about Meg
Since then, Meg has been clinging to Heidi and keeping a BIG distance from me. She wouldn't make eye contact, and the bigger distance she wanted, the lower she hangs her head, like saying, "Don't even get near me!" And at times her head is down as far as it will go onto her chest. However, don't let her fool you, for she is watching and listening to everything.

I still can't hold her, but it does seem she's relaxing a little more each day, though. Her eyes are getting brighter and she's smiling more all the time, too! Meg is also very, very thin. In watching her eat, we wonder, "Why?" She shovels the food in quickly with heaping spoonfuls and both kids eat a LOT. At this rate she'll catch up in no time unless there is a parasite we don't yet know about. We'll see!

Nik knows, since Meg claims Heidi for everything, he goes with me, taking my hand or letting me hold him or push him in the stroller. The kids are really awesome to take out, too. They barely fuss or cry at all.

Nik is saying quite a few English words if I ask him to repeat them after me. Sometimes he's calling me "Gammie" on his own, but also says such things as "good hug," "cow," "moo" (a boy after Grampa's heart, too), "dog," and many more.

I am again a very proud "Gammie."
These are great kids, too, like all our other grandkids. (26 altogether...and counting!) I am very much looking forward to seeing Nik and Meg blossom as time goes on. Thanks, Heidi and Mike, for giving me this opportunity for such a GREAT, GREAT experience!

After all, how many "Gammies" have such an experience as THIS?

HEIDI: I imagine Nik thinking, "Just because the gummy bear looks like candy doesn't mean it is!" Whereas, Meg would think, "If it looks like food, I'll take it!"

How anyone could hang their head right into their chest like Meg was nothing short of impressive. Her body language did all the talking. It screamed, "keep your distance, stay away!" Mom knew to win Meg's affection, though, a little at a time.

Nik took to "Gammie" right from the start. It was fun watching him interact with her as they looked at books and toys and her camera.

Mom's post reminds me how appreciative I am for her willingness and enthusiasm to travel with me to Kazakhstan. It was a big thing for her to leave her comfortable home in Maine to do this crazy trip!

The Good Life: Amplify
To say I have shared an experience such as this with my mother is marvelous. Besides Mike and me, she is the first to know Nik and Meg and she continues to be a significant and wonderful "Gammie!"

MIKE: *It's really interesting: the first time Nik saw me, I had a camera. And the first time he saw Gammie, she had a camera. Today, Nik plans to go to college for a degree in photography and videography.*

Meg has always loved being in Maine with Gammie, Grampie, and his cows.

50. Cries in the Night
& Twenty-Minute Waits

Posted by Heidi
Tuesday, September 21, 2004

Nap time went pretty well and, in the evening, Meg and Nik played together great. They played so great that they got into some baby powder. Their first mischievous act. They walked into the living area with powder all over them. They looked so funny. I took pictures but it does not do them justice.

At 10:30 it was bedtime. Or at least I thought so. Nik did not. He cried and wailed. I took him to the potty, which did not help. Mom thought Nik might be hungry, so we got both Nik and Meg out of bed and fed them. Maybe that is the problem. Nik quieted down after a bit.

I awake to cries in the night. It is Nik crying and wailing. What time is it anyway? 4 am! Maybe he will cry himself back to sleep? Ummm...no. At Mom's suggestion we gave him more food and he went potty two more times. That settled him down enough to go back to sleep.

Nik woke up this morning as happy as ever. As though last night did not happen. His Momma woke up with eyes red and smarting.

Mom and I decided that today we should get more groceries for the rest of the week. I called the office and arranged to be picked up at 11:30 am. After getting ready we went down our three flights of stairs. We waited for 20 minutes, which was unusual. We walked back up our three flights of stairs and called the office. It would be another 20 minutes. Our driver got stopped on the way here, oops.

After a quick snack for Meg and Nik, we went down the stairs to try again. Once at the Ramstore, Mom and I thought we had better eat lunch at a fast food place there. Unfortunately, "fast food" did not happen for us. "It will be three minutes." TWENTY minutes later it was ready. We eat and are finally ready to get the groceries.

Getting groceries is exhausting, before even factoring in being in a foreign country. I point and gesture to receive some food behind the counter. After paying and bagging the food ourselves, we are ready to go. Except that our driver, I guess, is not. We cart our food out to the car but Kostya is nowhere to be found. With eyes smarting from lack of sleep, I go back in, looking for him. About—you guessed it— twenty minutes later, he arrives. We have one hour when we finally return because we have an appointment with the US Embassy at 4 pm.

We put our groceries away, feed and potty Meg and Nik, and the hour is up. Down the stairs again, this time to the embassy. The interview went quickly and smoothly. People in the US Embassy were helpful, friendly, and English speaking. We met other adoptive parents while waiting, which was neat.

We now have Kazakhstan passports and American visas for Meg and Nik. And that is the final step! We are done! There is no reason we cannot go home. Okay, let's go!!!

But, wait (shall we say twenty minutes). I must be forgetting something. Oh yes, there is one drawback. In order to use Mike's frequent flyer miles, we will stay until the 26th. Four days from now. I am looking forward to getting home but I think the time here to get to know and understand Meg and Nik will be very helpful for when we do return home.

The biggest question for Mom and me, though, is…will we get sleep tonight?!?

Oh, I hope so!

HEIDI: Great fun was had walking back and forth through the apartment hallway from the living room at one end to the bedroom at the other transporting toys, books, papers and such. Along the route was the bathroom and baby powder. Not only were they covered, but the bathroom was, too!

Partners in Crime

For the next several years, if it was quiet too long, I knew those two were up to no good. They've been caught shoving as many toys as they could into the toilet bowl. Once, our central vac was found clogged with toys and clothes. There was a scary instance when Nik and Meg removed an outlet cover and Meg stuck an open barrette into both prongs of the outlet. She got the shock of her life that day!

Getting Nik and Meg on a synchronized sleeping schedule was becoming increasingly important. I was running on fumes! I don't know how I managed. Very seldom did both kids nap at the same time. I didn't sleep well with two children and whatever else was in the double bed. I remember feeling tired all the time but pushing myself by saying, "It's only a few more days. I can do this. When I get home I can rest."

There were only two activities planned that day and it was two too many!

The Good Life: Plot & Clarify

I'm glad we had those days in the Almaty apartment. It gave us a chance to get to know each other; to firm up a foundation for the new family we were going to build. It provided a cushion for Nik and Meg before traveling on a plane to a new home, a new country, three new siblings, before...so many new things.

51. Scary Faces & Pooping Discotheques

Posted by Heidi
Wednesday, September 22, 2004

I ended the last blog post by asking, "The biggest question for Mom and me, though, is...will we get sleep tonight?!?"

NO is the answer!

Nik fell asleep at 11 pm and woke up crying at midnight. Mom and I had fed Nik and Meg oatmeal at 10 pm so I knew he was not hungry. He cried, though, nice and loud. It almost appeared like a temper tantrum in his sleep. Two hours later he went back to sleep. It is so hard to figure out the possible reasons but I have a feeling this will be our new ritual for a while until he gets used to his new situation. One reason for this might be that he is crying for his caregiver. Maybe this is Nik's way to grieve.

Today we went to the Tsum. It is a big three-story store. It's not a department store, though. It's more like an inside bazaar. The first floor is electronics, the second floor clothing, and the third has household items and souvenirs. We stayed on the third floor for souvenirs. We walked from booth to booth with most of the same items in each one. If we lingered even a moment, the owners would show us all their wares. We managed to escape having purchased only a few items. We could not wait to get back. Nik decided he had

had enough and would not walk. We had lunch and napped for a couple of hours. Boy, did that feel good! We walked to Thomi's Pastry, which is a very long three blocks from here.

It is a discovery process with Meg and Nik. I bought a sandwich for them. Meg ate it with no problem. Nik took a little bite and decided he did not like the meat or the spread. This has happened a few times lately. So it seems Meg will eat whatever is offered whereas Nik is more finicky.

We walked "home" and fed the kids again and now they are playing. Meg and Nik go back and forth between "Gammie" and me, showing us their "scary" faces. They think this is the funniest thing.

Please don't let them scare you!

So much time is spent on eating and peeing and pooping. I must have conveniently blocked this from my memory with our other three children. Nik does very well using the potty chair on his own. Meg will only sometimes. They go quite frequently, though, which means I am emptying potty chairs several times a day. It's like a discotheque with Nik and Meg turning the light on and off while I'm trying to empty and clean the pots. Meg will usually start to poop while standing right beside me. I'll quickly get her to her potty chair where she finishes the job. I tried putting training pants on her this morning right after she had peed. I was then getting ready in the bathroom (Nik was turning the light on and off, of course) with Meg standing right behind me, which is where she peed through the training pants onto the floor. Back on goes the diaper.

Only three more days left in Almaty, Kazakhstan. Now that our paperwork is all done, Mike says Mom and I can vacation. We do hope to see a few sights in the next couple of days. I'll keep you posted!

HEIDI: Honestly, when I read these posts, I am reminded how tired I felt. It was really hard.

The Good Life: Clarify

But I pushed myself, knowing I needed to keep going because this experience, this time, would only happen once. It was important, and it would be worth it.

When I take a step back, I realize how crazy our schedule was. We hit the ground running, right after our long flights. Our first night in Kaz was on the overnight train to Taraz. Not even a full day in Taraz, and then we're back on the train to Almaty. From then on, it was Nik keeping us up every night. I truly don't know how we got through it.

The whole eating, peeing, and pooping was an all-consuming job. I had no idea just how long that would last. We used the potty chairs for months after we got home because Nik and Meg were too little to sit or stand at a regular toilet. They were so small! Meg's bottom was tiny. She had to hold herself up so she wouldn't fall in! Plus, the aforementioned mischievous acts showed that growth and maturity were needed before they could be trusted to use a bathroom for what it's actually for, not a toy repository!

52. Lunch in a Yurt

Posted by Heidi
Thursday, September 23, 2004

We have had perfect weather during this trip. It has been neither hot nor cold and has been sunny nearly every day. Only one night did it rain. The temperature in the apartment has also been just right.

A good day for the mountains, wouldn't you say? There was not a cloud in the sky. Off we go. We stopped two times on the way up for the scenery and pictures. We had a great view of the mountains. We opted not to go on the chair lift, though, for two small but obvious reasons. Especially since Nik seemed to find the stairs more than he could handle. He sat down on the ground in protest. He was carried the rest of the way to the car.

I asked to be taken to the Aul "Aool" restaurant where Kazakh food is served in yurts. I was told beforehand they had a menu in English but, alas, they did not. Kostya, our driver, came to our aid. Yet, with his limited English and my limited Kazak, he recommended only one dish. He said it was the best one from the list. Maybe you can guess which meal this might be. Yes, indeed, it is the dish with horse meat.

Kostya thought we should have three orders and also tea with milk. Really...how can Mom leave Kazakhstan without having horse meat?!?

The temperature was cool in the yurt. Colorful and vibrant rugs covered the walls. Our round table sat low to the ground and had square seats with no backs. We were the only ones there. Maybe they don't get too many people this time of year. Mom handled the horse meat quite well, even though we both agree it has a gamey taste. Meg and Nik ate it right up. Surprisingly, we consumed all three plates! And so, with another new experience under our belts, we are ready to go "home."

An outing that may be only a few hours is tiring. We are always glad to get back. I think Meg and Nik are, too. Last night went better with Nik. After eating our 10:30 pm meal, we were ready for bed at 11 pm. 11 pm is better than midnight. Nik wanted two toys to take to bed but I said one. He did not want to choose and this set off his crying spell. He cried for an hour or so and then settled down to sleep and, fortunately, did not wake up the rest of the night.

After a nap Mom and I decided to go to Thomi's again with hopes to also stop at a little supermarket nearby that hadn't had electricity the day before. This excursion was not an easy feat. We thought it would be easier to maneuver with one stroller and, since Nik did not seem to want to walk, we put him in it. He did not agree and began to carry on. Okay then, we put Meg in the stroller instead. I felt he should walk, which he did some, but he fussed most of the way there.

After Thomi's we went to the market. Nik was carrying on again and would not walk so I picked him up. As soon as Meg saw this, she plopped down on the floor crying and would not stand up. Mom went to get a grocery cart while they continued on. Even with both of them placed in the cart, it was touch and go. We clearly did not stay long. Upon exiting the store we put Nik in the stroller and both kids were completely fine. Mom and I were not, though. We keep trying to figure out how to best deal with these behaviors with thoughts of our long...long trip back to the states.

We are not sure of tomorrow's plan yet. We'll let you know.

HEIDI: An excursion to the mountains in all its expansiveness and with few people around seemed worth a try. Can't beat being out in the open on a beautiful day! I am glad we made the effort but it was frustrating not knowing why or when Nik and Meg would cry. It seemed that Nik would decide at some point he'd walked enough. He'd sit down or cry or both. Why? Do kids not walk much in the baby home? Is he in pain? I had no clue what was triggering this.

What are Yurts for?
Kazakhs are a nomadic people historically, and a yurt is a much nicer version of a tent. It can be dismantled and moved from one location to the next but, unlike a tent, a yurt is actually a home, with whole families living in them. We took a lot of pictures. I knew Nik and Meg would not remember any of this, but at least they would have the pictures.

Nik, Meg, and I slept together in a double bed while in the Almaty apartment. Sleeping with newly adopted young children is recommended for building attachment and bonding in the parent/child relationship. There is only so much room in one bed, though. Since the kids and I were not leaving, some toys must! That's why I had Nik choose one toy, not two. I don't know if it was worth all the crying, though.

I remember feeling very discouraged when I wrote this post. It was a very long trip to get back home to the states and we were just days from leaving. What would we do if Nik and Meg cried on the planes and couldn't be consoled? How would we manage two kids in strollers and all our carry-ons during layovers and from one flight to the next?

How would the four of us get home in one piece if we couldn't even get to the grocery store without incident?

53. Walking Tour of Almaty

Posted by Heidi
Friday, September 24, 2004

SPECIAL BULLETIN: Today is Mike's and my 16th anniversary. Happy Anniversary, Mike. I love you!

Today we used both strollers to go to Panfilov Park. There is a Russian Orthodox Church, a WWII memorial and a couple of museums. To get there, we passed the Green Market then strolled through the Silk Way City (a modern mall) and ended our walking tour at the Tsum. Here we bought a few more souvenirs. Meg and Nik were quite well behaved until the end. We had five blocks uphill from the Tsum to get "home." The kids had to walk the last bit because there are a lot of stairs. (Rather than crossing the street at some intersections, they have underground tunnels we could use.) By the end, both children were crying.

They were tired so I fed them and then laid down. This time it was Meg who woke up whimpering after only a short time. This woke Nik up and, given time, Meg wore off on Nik and he began crying, too. I brought them to the kitchen where I gave Nik a drink and that's when we encountered our first "tumble."

Nik fell off the chair onto the floor. He hit his forehead with his cup and the back of his head on the floor. "Gammie" put ice on his boo-

boos and held him until he calmed down. Meg continued to cry during this whole episode. I offered her a drink but she kept refusing and turning away. Eventually she inched her way closer to the table, stopped crying and began to eat and drink. Nik seems fine now. It was a bit of a scare for all of us, though.

Through this week Nik has acquired a plastic bag and has added to it each day. He has also found another round toy to put things in. His treasure chests include paper, napkins, some items from the kitchen, pictures, and miscellaneous toys. He definitely enjoys collecting things. Nik also has a children's book that shows fish, balls, cows, and bunny rabbits. He walks around with this book and takes it to bed. Nik will point to a picture. Mom or I will tell him what it is and then he tries to repeat the word. While I read in bed he will look at his book. He has learned many English words already. He just soaks it in.

There are three or four good-sized stuffed animals here. One is about as big as they are, if not bigger. Meg and Nik will take the stuffed mouse from the shelf, hit it, and drag it around the apartment in what appears to be attempts to conquer this bigger-than-life animal. The kids have also had great fun with empty soda and water bottles. They carry them around, banging them on walls and doors. It is so cute when they are playing  and they jibber jabber back and forth, totally involved in their game. I do wish at these times that I could understand what they are saying.

Even now Meg has put toys on two chairs and seems to be instructing her "pupils." She is also showing them a picture of Zack that she carries around. Meg likes to make sure everything is in its place, right down to every scrap of paper she finds to be thrown away. The biggest problem Meg has is...keeping her pants up! She has a pullup on with a safety pin holding it on and yet...it is hanging down to her knees! Over time, they fall to her ankles. Not much fun when you are trying to play!

We have been keeping the oddest hours here. Usually Mom and I are up until 1 or 2 am and then we get up again between 8 and 9 am.

In the afternoons the kids nap and sometimes Mom and I will, too. We are hoping this will be to our advantage on the trip home. On the 26th (tomorrow night), we leave the apartment at 1:10 am with our flight from Almaty to Frankfurt leaving at 4:20 am. Mom and I are hoping we can all take a late afternoon nap tomorrow and sleep as long as we can so we'll be somewhat rested and, by the time we get on the plane, we'll all be ready to sleep. Of course we are hoping Meg and Nik will cooperate with our intricately laid out plan. We can only hope and pray!

— NOW —

HEIDI: It was important that Nik and Meg get used to the strollers in anticipation of our upcoming travels. Our walks allowed us to do that and see our neighborhood, too.

How do you dial 911 in Kazakhstan? Visions of Nik in an Almaty hospital with our long awaited travel plans going up in smoke raced through my mind. You can imagine my relief when Nik emerged fairly unscathed from this incident.

I loved watching Nik and Meg play together. Oh, to know what they were saying!

I decided Meg needed to stay in diapers until we could concentrate on potty training at home. I mentioned in the beginning how I was told she and Nik were potty trained. Obviously she was not. I bought pull-ups for her but even the smallest ones did not work. They simply would not stay on her tiny form. Finding the right-sized diaper became my mission. I certainly did not want any of the potential disasters I was envisioning happening on our travels home.

MIKE: *Right around this time, I headed to Florida for a business trip. I remember sitting on my colleague's hotel balcony with him on a warm night, trying to explain how my life had changed since I last saw him.*

Where in the world could I begin? He had been living his normal life, running a business, working with clients, doing errands, and eating at restaurants. Meanwhile, I had been in Kazakhstan adopting two kids!

As we talked that night, I found our conversation...lacking. It wasn't his fault. It was simply the fact that what drove me, and what gave me purpose the last time we talked, was no longer as important to me.

The Good Life: Own

I realize now how that night was a turning point. I couldn't simply go "back" to my old way of life. It wouldn't be too long before my career began to lose some of its luster. I was clearly moving in a new direction, one that helped me make more of a difference in the world and not simply make money. I didn't realize it at the time, but my old life didn't fit me anymore.

This adoption was growing a heart.

54. The Politics of Packing

Saturday, 25, September 2004
Posted by Heidi

The four of us have had a pretty good week here in Almaty. We spent today packing. Meg and Nik cooperated with a late nap and are still sleeping at 8:15. I slept an hour but Mom was unable to sleep.

I wonder what Meg and Nik will think about all that is about to take place. Their lives will be quite different. A life in Kazakhstan vs. a life in the United States. We have tried to prepare them to see "Poppa," Zack, Jake, and Brynn, as well as flying on a plane. I just don't know how much they grasp of this. I especially wonder how they will react when they see Zack, Jake, and Brynn in real life! Nik and Meg look at their pictures and say their names and have said "hi" to them on the phone. No matter how they respond, I am so looking forward to their first meeting.

With the exception of ten days at home I have been in Kazakhstan for most of August and September. That's quite a while to be away. The longest I've ever been away, that's for sure.

I'm grateful for the time and experiences here yet I am also grateful to get back home. With two more children to boot!

The Good Life: Power & Presence

HEIDI: My anxiety and nervousness went into the background
once I was in travel mode. I had no time to worry; I had to get
this packing right!

This was it. For the last time, I was packing up. The mental checklist
was dizzying:

- Where would I keep the important documents, passports, flight information, etc. so they were safe?

- What items would Mom have with her and what backup information should she have in case we were separated?

- Should we have a bag for Nik and a bag for Meg? That way if I had Meg (which would most likely be the case), I would have her bag and Mom would have Nik and his bag.

- What items needed to be easily accessible in each bag?

- Would we actually be able to maneuver and get around with all our bags? We were allowed two pieces of carry-on luggage and one small bag each back then. That could be up to twelve pieces all together plus two umbrella strollers!

- And managing two kids, of course!?

I packed very strategically, knowing exactly the size and weight and
number of bags allowed.

I did not want to check our luggage because going to baggage claim
would take more time and require more walking/strolling between
flights. I knew it would be a lot to carry but conversely it would avoid
extra hassle, confusion, and problems, with less of a chance of losing
luggage, too. After spending the day packing, our luggage was finally
set and ready to go.

Or so we thought.

55. Oh, the Wonders of Travel

Sunday, September 26, 2004
Posted by Heidi

Yes, we did get home safely!

I am so glad to be here. It is hard to believe after being with Meg and Nik in Kazakhstan that they are now right here in our home.

But let's back up and talk about our crazy travels to get us here.

The following details the 30+ hour journey home:

Packing and Repacking
The evening before we left the apartment, a person that works for the adoption agency asked if we would take some traditional Kazakh items to the states and mail it from there to Ohio and Virginia. Kazakh adoptees wanted their adopted children to see more of the Kazakh culture at their adoption reunions.

Now this posed a bit of a problem. My strategy had been to not check any luggage, so I said we could probably fit a few things into one of our backpacks. I was not quite sure we fully understood each other on the phone, but he would come at 8:30 pm and we would figure things out then.

I was taken aback when a huge bag came through the door weighing right at the 40-pound limit! It was hard to say no. The package was for a good cause but there was no way I could maneuver all this stuff. We had two children (of course), two strollers, two backpacks, two rolling backpacks, and two smaller

bags. Mom and I decided we should do this but only if we knew for sure the package would be checked straight to Boston. Sasha, our contact, agreed to meet us at the airport and make sure it would be checked straight through.

Mom and I wondered what we were getting ourselves into. Now that we were checking a bag, though, we might as well check more. By 11 pm we had repacked so we could also check our two rolling backpacks if we wanted to.

After that we showered and got the kids fed and ready. Mom laid down for a few minutes before we left at 1:10 am.

The Almaty Airport

We met Sasha at the airport. The desk person said the package would indeed be sent straight through to Boston. Once Mom and I were sure of this, we checked in our two other pieces. Sasha was a big help in getting boarding passes for all three flights and getting us in front of the long line at passport control since we were flying with two children.

We waited to board the plane at 3:30 am. Once on the plane, I looked at the seats and kicked myself for not having picked up on this at the ticket counter. We had four seats in four different places! I wanted four seats in the middle so Mom and I could help each other. I did ask some other passengers, and they were kind enough to get us closer together. We ended up on the right side of the plane with two seats in front of each other, plus a person seated to our left. Mom had Nik because Meg would cry if she was not with me. Meg and I sat behind Mom and Nik.

The Frustrating Flight to Frankfurt

This flight was seven hours and it was close to the nightmare I had imagined! I'm sure it was also a nightmare for all the passengers surrounding us! Nik basically threw his temper tantrums at frequent intervals throughout the flight. Mom tried to console him at first and then I took him in my seat. Nothing helped. I just let him cry and scream and did my best to minimize the ominous decibel level. This flight was through the night when most passengers were trying to sleep. Having virtually no sleep myself I decided I could not look too far ahead. I needed to deal with only what was directly in front of me. Baby steps, again. Next up, the six hour layover in Frankfurt.

The Long Layover

Mom and I noticed—from a map of the airport—a kids play section that was in another terminal. When we found it we realized getting there would require going through security. We decided it wasn't

worth the effort or the risk. Instead, we went to our gate and waited there the rest of the time. My main goal during our layover was keeping Meg and Nik awake. Maybe then they would sleep on the next flight. For some reason, even with our boarding passes, we had to go through three separate lines to get to our gate. Somewhere in those three lines, Meg and Nik couldn't take it anymore and fell asleep.

We had to wake them to board the plane. They both began to cry and, before we were even seated, a temper tantrum by Nik began. I had Benadryl with me and decided to give him half a dose. It was worth a try. Nik's behavior could not be worse. Could it?

Flight Two: Frankfurt to Pittsburgh

We settled in our seats, the plane began to move and then, it stopped. The pilot announced there was a mechanical problem that would now be assessed. He'd keep us posted. The problem added an extra hour to our already nine-hour flight. And, this delay almost guaranteed us missing our connecting flight.

If the first flight was a nightmare, though, then this one was a dream! Nik was so much better behaved and both kids slept for a long period, allowing a very tired Momma to get some sleep. I held Meg this time while Nik slept partially beside Mom and partially with Mom. Ten hours is a long trip but it felt good knowing we were landing on US soil.

Eventually Flight Three: Pittsburgh to Boston

Mom and I were hoping against all hope to make our next flight. We quickly got off the plane but, from there, everything pretty much went straight downhill. We waited and waited for the strollers. Everyone on our flight was ahead of us when we finally got them. We were last in the long line for Immigration. We knew then we'd miss our flight. After Immigration, we were taken to a side office where the adoption documents were provided and Meg and Nik's Kazakh visas were stamped.

Another thing. Before we landed, we were informed that we would have to get our checked luggage and recheck it! *Are you kidding me?* I debated whether to leave the bags and hope they would somehow make it to Boston but then thought better of that. I got a cart and piled all the luggage on—including that huge 40-pound package! When I took Meg from her stroller and put her on the cart, she put up quite a fuss so I tried to simultaneously hold her and steer the cart. Mom had three bags and Nik in a stroller. The next long line was for our declaration forms and, after that, the line to recheck our luggage.

Should we try to get to Boston or see about flights to Portland?

"Where are your bags going, ma'am?"

"I don't know because we missed our flight."

The guy went away and came back saying there was a 5:30 pm flight to Boston. "Okay then, let's go to Boston!"

Mom had her cell phone so we could contact Mike. Now that we knew when we were flying and where, we tried to call him. Why the phone wouldn't work we'll never know. We made sure it was charged before leaving Kazakhstan. With no extra time to use a pay phone, we were not able to get in touch with Mike before leaving Pittsburgh.

After the man at the desk took our baggage, we went through yet another security line and, with no restroom break, we made it to the gate just in time. There was a disconcerting moment when the boarding attendant was not sure if there were enough seats for us on the plane. It was a relief when she returned with four boarding passes.

Fortunately, Nik and Meg slept most of this short flight. Best of all, only one and a half more hours before we'd meet Mike in Boston! Mike was returning from a business trip in Florida and was to arrive in Boston about the same time we were arriving. Of course, because we were flying in later, surely he would be waiting for us.

The Disappointing Arrival
Well, Mike was not there to meet us when we arrived in Boston. Maybe baggage claim? No.

Now what?

I did not want to get our checked luggage until I knew what was going on. The luggage guy said he would keep it there for us. I then went to USAir to check on Mike's flight from Florida. I could not find his flight. Next, I used a payphone to call my father. No answer. I then tried calling my sister, Amy, collect but was informed these numbers were blocked. Now what?

Then, it occurred to me, I could call Mike's cell phone. He answered! But, oh no, because of a *hurricane* in Florida he was still there. Yes. A hurricane. He would not be meeting us.

Mike was able to arrange for a driver with a van to pick us up at the airport and take us to Portsmouth, New Hampshire. Mike had also talked with my father who would now be waiting to pick us up in Portsmouth. This trip was not over yet!

I found the driver and then went back to retrieve the checked luggage. Mom got the car seats in place and the kids buckled up while I managed to get two pieces of luggage and the 40-pound monstrosity on one of our strollers, and somehow get it all up an escalator and out the door to the van.

The One-Plus-Two Hours of Driving

In one hour we met Dad and my brother, Seth. Boy, was it nice to see them! Once the transfer was made, Dad drove the remaining two hours to get us home. Mike had planned to surprise Mom and me by meeting us in Pittsburgh and, from there, we'd have all flown to Boston together. Instead, he was stuck in Florida and would probably not get home until Tuesday. I was disappointed. I'd envisioned a homecoming *with* Mike, not without him. Mike would now miss seeing Nik and Meg and they, in turn, would not see their Poppa when they first arrived home.

I have to say though, I have such an amazing mother! She was that leaf in a stream. She took all the happenings in stride throughout our adventure. She picked up the slack when it was needed and helped when help was needed. I can't thank you enough, Mom! I love you!

Home!

We arrived home at 11:30 pm. Zack, Jake, and Brynn were awaiting our arrival along with my sister, Amy, and her husband, Peter. Meg and Nik were woken up. They were not very social, which was not surprising given they were probably more scared and disoriented than anything. We visited a few minutes and then Mom, Dad, and Seth said good-bye. It was then that Nik began to really cry. Mom and I realized right away that Nik would not understand why

"Gammie" was leaving.

After they left, I called Mike and got the scoop on what happened (he said he'll tell "the rest of the story" himself in a later post).

Amy and Peter then said their good-byes. I will be forever grateful to Amy and Peter for their willingness to watch our kids during these two trips!

It was about 1 am before we got settled for bed. All the kids slept on the floor in my bedroom. I did not think Meg and Nik would sleep because they had slept so much beforehand. So I was pleased when they both did sleep through the night with the exception of Nik having to go to the bathroom one time. I got some much-needed sleep!

It is tough to describe emotions and feelings yet. I guess I'm just finding it hard to believe that we have finally completed this adoption journey. I see Meg and Nik here, yet it doesn't really seem real. It will sink in soon, I'm sure. I am so looking forward to adjusting and raising our FIVE children!

Thanks to all of you, for your care, your thoughts, and your prayers! I know you agree that Meg and Nik are worth all of them!

— NOW —

HEIDI: Man, when I think of the hurdles it took to get home, I wonder how we did it.

- ✓ Too much luggage
- ✓ Up all night
- ✓ Flying all night
- ✓ Seats not together
- ✓ Nonstop crying
- ✓ A six-hour layover
- ✓ A delayed flight
- ✓ Missing the connecting flight
- ✓ Manually checking and rechecking luggage
- ✓ A hurricane
- ✓ No Mike in Boston…No Mike for two more days!

There's more, but I think that's a long enough list!

Yeah, I was pretty devastated when Mike was not there to meet us in Boston. I was glad he was okay but this was not the homecoming I'd imagined (and, believe me, I had imagined it many times). I'd thought again and again how relieved I'd be to finally see him. Any reserves I had were practically gone, yet somehow I would have to find a little more for a little longer.

I had doctors' appointments scheduled for the very next morning. There was no way I could go to an appointment with five kids all by myself. Plan B had to be figured out before I even arrived home.

My sister, Amy, and brother-in-law, Peter, along with Zack, Jake, and Brynn had eagerly been waiting. Because of our delays it was a much later night. Despite the tiredness, it was a joy to see them again!

Amy and Peter are not mentioned much in the blog but they were absolutely pivotal to the success of this adoption. Mike and I knew our three kids were in good hands with them. I expect suddenly being responsible for three children turned their world upside-down! I'm so grateful for their sacrifice in order to expand the Vayda family. Turns out it was good practice. They now have SIX kids of their own!

MIKE: I'm a bit shocked to find that I never wrote that post telling my side of the story of the arrival. Here's the sad, frustrating story:

While I was in Florida, I had this brilliant idea to surprise Heidi in Pittsburgh, where they were catching their connecting flight. I managed to change my flights to go through Pittsburgh and then get on the same flight as them to Boston. I pictured how happy she would be to see me there. I pictured Nik and Meg's eyes as they recognized their Poppa and ran to give me a hug. I pictured the crowds of people with tears in their eyes at the reunion.

Man, it was gonna be good!

I was going to arrive in plenty of time to meet them as they got off the plane. I was so excited to be able to surprise her, especially because I knew it would be a big help to her to travel the rest of the way with them.

And then Hurricane Charley decided to take an unexpected detour to the west coast of Florida. Try as I might, I could not get a flight out! In fact, they informed me I was going to be delayed by several days. I was so frustrated. I was on the phone with many supervisors, but, even though I was top of the heap as a frequent flyer, they couldn't get me out of there.

It was a huge disappointment. Huge. I lay in bed in my top floor suite, listening to the roar of the rain lash my sliding glass door all night long, thinking about how wrong it was that I would not be there the first night my two kids came home.

To this day, it makes me sad. For all the moments of grace we experienced throughout the trip...this was not one of them. I regret not being there to help Heidi. I regret not being any assistance whatsoever during an incredibly difficult time. Most of all, I deeply regret not being in our bed that first night with my family. I feel like I let them down. I know it wasn't my fault, but it doesn't make it any better. Definitely the biggest disappointment of the whole journey.

The only saving grace was getting an earlier flight than I expected. I have a clear memory of arriving late at night, walking into the bedroom, and seeing all five of my kids sleeping together on the floor.

All five.

I stood there watching them for a long time.

Questions to consider
What were some of the sacrifices Mike & Heidi made in "Off you go...again"? Have you made sacrifices in your life for the greater Good? What were they? What did you get in return?
(For more questions and your **free** study guide,
go to **NotFar.org/Kaz)**

Part 6

Brave new world

56. Our First Days in the U.S.A.

Tuesday, 28, September 2004
Posted by Heidi

Today marks a birthday...mine! Thirty nine years old and feeling it, too! (Or maybe it's the jet lag and the time change. Hard to say.) Here's a quick recap on our first two days home.

Monday
After finally arriving so late the night before...and not having Mike here...we still needed to be up and going first thing. We head to the appointments I'd scheduled for Nik and Meg at the doctor's office. Mom took me and all five kids. Zack, Jake, and Brynn have waited so long to see Meg and Nik and wanted to be with them every minute. Understandable. The doctor's visit went as well as could be expected. Both Meg and Nik received five shots and, in a few days, they will need to go to the hospital for lab work.

The next item on the agenda was to get this big package off our hands. We went to Mailboxes Etc. and the burden was lifted! After a Burger King drive-thru stop we came home. We had naptime for almost all six of us and then had visitors stop by later in the afternoon.

Tuesday

Mike managed to find an earlier flight and got home at 1:30 am this morning. Meg and Nik were surprised to find "Poppa" here when they woke up.

Then, we had a surprise birthday party for me...in the woods! It was a really creative and fun way to celebrate my first birthday as a mother of FIVE! I missed the woods around our house while we were gone, so it was a great gift.

So how do I feel?

Aside from exhausted, it's hard to put into words. I think right now, we're just trying to put one foot in front of the other and do the very next thing we have to do. I haven't really tried to process the enormity of the changes in our family, or all that we've accomplished.

At this point? It's all about baby steps!

HEIDI: I can't believe how much there was to do and how we got through it all! Maybe scheduling a doctor's visit the very first day home was not the best idea. I'm sure there were reasons why I did this but I don't recall what they are now. It seems like these appointments could have been put off at least a day or two.

Shots all around!

It was highly recommended that immunizations be given as soon as possible due to the questionable quality and actual issuance of the original immunizations. It sure didn't make our first few days easy, though!

Fortunately, Mom was willing to drive us to the city and helped with all the kids. Monday's appointments felt never ending. I just wanted to be home.

Immunizations. What a way to begin a new life. Welcome to the USA!

57. Drawing Blood Draws Screams

Wednesday, September 29, 2004
Posted by Mike

Hey, who wants to have some fun? You say you do? Then you simply *must* take your adopted Kazakh kids to get blood work done!

As we headed for the hospital, we realized that there's just no way you can prepare them for what's to come. How do you pantomime drawing blood—at least in a way that doesn't scare them to death? In the end, you just decide to surprise them. Fun surprise. Woo-hoo.

I'm finding that I'm becoming less dependent on what others think of me as a result of this adoption (you should see the looks I get when I tell people I have FIVE kids). It's a good thing, too. Because, when one of them is screaming bloody murder from a room way down the hall, and you hear in the waiting room—as do the rest of the people waiting with you—you can just sit back and shrug.

And, best of all, when the child you are holding in the waiting room decides that he, too, must join in and support his sister in her time of need by screaming right along with her, well, what better time to tell yourself, Who cares what anyone else thinks? I LIKE the screaming!

We made it through. But it was a tough one. You thought drawing blood from a turnip was hard? Try two Kazakhs.

HEIDI: Yup. Back to the city again. This time for blood work. Though all this made logical sense, Mike and I felt bad. Nik and Meg already had far more than their share of painful experiences in their short lives.

MIKE: *I'd always been overly concerned with what others thought of me. Maybe it was because I was raised a Preacher's Kid. I felt I was always on stage, since my dad's job security kind of depended on it. (I did a horrendous job of helping him stay employed, by the way.)*

I mentioned back at the beginning of the book, when we were doing our required adoption weekend, that it hit me for the first time that my family would be a minority family. And the weeks in Kazakhstan did help to get me used to that fact.

Still, when we started going out into the American world as a multi-racial family of seven, in the very white state of Maine, I felt that everyone was staring. I imagined the comments. It wasn't very fun.

I think it reminded me of how I felt to be in the spotlight as a child again. Thinking that everyone was watching me and my actions. But I'm happy to say that it didn't take too long for me to get over that feeling!

The Good Life: Own

That day in the doctor's office helped quite a bit. You can only be embarrassed for so long until, as I wrote, you simply shrug. Those kids were over-the-top dramatic about that blood work. I know my parenting skills were put to test that day. They got their blood drawn, and I kept my commitment to being their father. I call that a win-win!

58. The Quest for Poop

Friday, October 1, 2004
Posted by Mike

For ancient heroes (like King Arthur and Monty Python and Indiana Jones), seeking for the Holy Grail was a worthy endeavor. For others, seeking Truth, or pursuing Beauty was the goal. For the Vayda Family, it is a different quest.

We have chosen The Crusade for Crap.

Wednesday's trip to the hospital was all you could ask for in an adventure—and more. The screaming, the wailing, the panic and terror—oh, it was a wonderful experience. But it was only half of the adventure.

Our quest, which was given to us as we left on Wednesday, was to deliver back to the hospital some poop. Not just any old poop, though. Fresh poop. How fresh? It had to be less than one hour old.

I am not making this up, folks.

They say it was for testing. They say it was necessary to determine the health of the children.

I say it's just one more sick little joke in this ongoing bizarro world of adoption. Sure, the nurse *seems* professional. But I know that she just happened to be the one who got the short straw. She had to talk

232

to us and keep a straight face while the rest of her co-workers were behind the door rolling on the floor in helpless laughter. She reminded me of the evil nurse in *One Flew Over the Cuckoo's Nest*.

"Yes, that's correct. You need to deliver the stool to us here at the clinic within one hour of the movement. Pardon? Yes, Mr. Vayda, that's correct. Oh, and we need that for both of the children."

And we? We believed her.

So, yes, we did it. We followed the two kids around. We waited. And when they, er, *went*, my lovely wife was right there to...gather the...specimens. Then, off we go! The clock is ticking and we are still 40 minutes away from the lab!

"Now, we have to leave now!!" Heidi screams. "Let's go let's GO move Move MOVE!!"

We gather all the children, shoes trailing behind, strap two into seatbelts, wrestle two more into car seats, and proceed to drive wildly down our driveway and out towards our goal.

This, my friends, is the real *Amazing Race*.

We made it, in time. We raced in, breathless, two kids jabbering Kazakh in our arms, Jake and Brynn running behind.

We delivered the materials as requested.

And as the doors slid shut behind us, I swear I heard muffled peals of laughter.

So. Our life has come to this, has it?

A quest for crap, eh?

So be it.

You may laugh, Nurse Ratched.

But we'll wear these stains proudly. Because holy crap; we are *adoptive parents*.

HEIDI: The sheer craziness of it all is funny...now. It takes an hour to get to the city and back, then add an appointment and, just like that, half a day is gone. I had taken that drive three days in a row since my return so I sure was glad when we were able to make one, not two fast and furious trips because Nik and Meg happened to poop about the same time that day.

Remember back in Taraz when I bought those potty chairs? For months those chairs were a centerpiece in our great room. Nik and Meg could not easily get up onto a regular toilet and, even if they did, they were at risk of falling in because they were so small. They also could not be trusted to be alone and out of my sight (e.g., the baby powder incident). IF I had let them use the toilet I might just as well have packed up my clothes and moved into the bathroom because they were peeing and pooping all the time! I can see them now running from wherever they were to their potty chair, quickly pulling down their pants (if they had any on) to do their business. If they pooped they'd stand up and lean forward for someone to wipe their bottom. Even Brynn remembers this well. She did her share of bottom wiping back then.

Meg took quite a while to potty train. I tried pull ups, training pants and even wearing nothing to encourage peeing in the right place. They'd often sit on the potty chairs leaving "no business" behind. I was checking and carting these potty chairs to the bathroom to empty and clean and return umpteen times a day.

The scheduled appointment was to determine if Nik and Meg were carrying parasites. This is not uncommon for children from foreign countries. If parasites exist, medication is prescribed to eliminate them. Our two children were NOT exceptions. They needed it too.

MIKE: *First the bloodwork, then the poop parade. In a few months, I had gone from traveling the world on planes, coaching CEOs and managing six-figure budgets...to traveling to doctors in a minivan, coaching Kazakhs to poop and managing specimens of feces. It was a humbling experience, to say the least.*

The Good Life: Clarify
It was part of the process of changing me as a person, and changing my priorities forever. That, of course, is a really good thing. What was really, truly important? Giving up five-star resorts in the Swiss Alps was a big price to pay for enlightenment. I know it was a worthwhile trade.

59. Adoption Cookout

Sunday, October 3, 2004
Posted by Mike

Today we enjoyed a beautiful day at the ocean. We attended an adoption cookout. Basically, an adoption cookout is where you show up and adopt a hamburger and condiment of your choice. It's a huge commitment, of course. How do you know you'll still want that jar of Grey Poupon in a month, after the newness wears off?!

Actually, it was a chance to meet other families who have adopted (children, not burgers) through the same agency. Neither of us wanted to go. It had been a long week, and socializing with strangers is the last thing we want to do on the best of days. But we worked hard not to talk each other out of it and just packed everyone up and went.

It helped that the day was so beautiful. It was one of those days where you look around and think, "Wow. This is why people come to Maine."

It turned out to be a great experience. As we met different people, and we swapped stories, they all had a similar word of encouragement for us: "What? You've only been home a week?! What the heck are you DOING here?!?"

It made us take a step back and realize, you know, it may seem like

235

six years, but it's only been six days. True, it's been six days of non-stop noise, dropping things, pooping, saying "No!" approximately infinity times, crying, wailing, stubbornness, sleeplessness, Kazakh ramblings, puzzled looks, pooping, poutings, and of course, pooping. It feels like forever. (Maybe this is what Forever Family means?) But, it helped us to realize that we've only just begun.

"We've only just begun."

White lace and promises...a kiss for luck a...

(Sorry. Got lost in a Karen Carpenter moment there.)

Meeting these other families was really cool. To look around and see all these multicultural families was invigorating. Children from China, Guatemala, Nepal, and our little Kazakhs running around happily, seemingly carefree. It meant all the more when you yourself had seen where they'd come from, not that long ago. It was literally a picture of hope.

Amazing what a little sunlight can do for you.

HEIDI: The adoption picnic was our first official family outing. The weather was perfect with full sun and blue skies. The mark of a successful day is when everyone in the family has a good time. This was one of those days. We met several seasoned adoptive parents who were very encouraging to Mike and me. They knew firsthand the transition we were going through, having just arrived home with Nik and Meg. Even though we had a fairly frazzling first week at home, the picnic allowed us to take a step back to see how far we had come in our adoption adventure.

MIKE: I mentioned how that first night of the Florida business trip was a milestone on this journey for me; one that I couldn't recognize at the time. This picnic was another one.

It was very helpful to see other families like my new one. Many colors, races, cultures. There was a different feel to that day. It was full of people who were living an alternate life than the American norm. I really liked that feeling.

The Good Life: Presence

I do like being a rebel. I feel I'm at my best when I have an enemy to fight. I saw how our new family was an act of rebellion (so to speak). We brought two orphans into our family. We were choosing not to spend our resources and our life on buying bigger homes, better cars, and nicer stuff. We were now on a different path, and it was going against the tide. It felt good.

It wasn't possible to comprehend what our new life would mean, just six days in. But it certainly helped to see that encouragement all around me.

On our new path, we weren't alone.

60. A Unique Birthday

Monday, October 4, 2004
Posted by Mike

Once you get past 40 (and I'm not saying I am), birthdays kinda start seeming the same. There's no drama like in the 30s, no crisis of 39, no panic of the Big Four-Oh, no depression of 41. It's just one more of those birthdays.

Still, my birthday today was a pretty good one. It was a stunning fall day, and I took full advantage of it by getting outside as much as possible. My suddenly huge family threw me a great little party. Heidi's mother and father actually pried Meg off of Heidi and gave us two whole hours alone together. Since it takes 30 minutes to get anywhere, we wisely decided to stay at home and enjoy 100 minutes of blissful silence (They didn't make it for the whole two hours. But we *takes* what we can *gets*.)

I wish I could say we used those 100 minutes to solve the world's problems. Instead, we just kinda sat there, looking at each other and shaking our heads. We're just a few days into this new life, and what little brain power we have has been used up in just getting things done, and re-connecting with our three long-suffering older kids.

The three of them have been such awesome kids throughout the whole journey. I'm so glad to be able to see them, hug them, and toss the football with them again.

Finally, we finished the day with margaritas all around. Those three long-suffering older kids, Zack, Jake, and Brynn, really enjoyed them—even without Tequila!

The picture at the top speaks volumes about our life, and how it has changed since my last birthday. Never would I have guessed I'd have five children crowding around me on my 42nd birthday—all mine. And that two of them were fresh from a country halfway around the world? Come on.

I've got a pretty good imagination, but who could've ever dreamed up this?!

Maine margaritas. They've earned them!

MIKE: *I see the picture of those little kids huddled around me, and it makes me feel nostalgic for a different time. A time when I was a lot younger, wealthier, healthier, and my kids, who are now grown, were so little and dependent on me. My role as a father has changed so much since then.*

Now, as we begin to navigate the empty nest in our lives, I look at that picture and wonder, Did I do enough as their father? Enough to equip them for the world? Only time will tell.

But to be honest, I do not wish I could go back to that time. I treasure it for what it was, and I accept and appreciate now for what it is. And I am very glad we aren't still dealing with the challenges we had back then!

The Good Life: Plot

I can look back at the years of parenting since the adoption, and though I have doubts, I also have peace that we chose the right path. We changed the plot, and I'm so happy we did.

61. Baby Steps

Tuesday, October 5, 2004
Posted by Mike

It's Tuesday evening, and it's been a long day.

The whole family is here in the great room. Zack and Jake are working on a geography program I downloaded (Pretty fun, too. The fact that they're doing it on their own time is saying something).

Heidi is going through winter clothes with Brynn. Somehow, all the clothes shrunk over the past year. Or maybe the kids all grew like weeds. But a lot of the clothes are just NOT fitting.

Meg and Nik are wandering around, actually being, oh, *not* uncontrollable for a change.

Dad just got his new laptop via the FedEx man and is trying it out writing this. (So far, he's disappointed in it and having severe buyer's remorse. But that's another story.)

As we enter week two of being home, what one comment can we make with certainty?

We are astounded—stunned—at the stubbornness of these two kids.

Don't let these little faces of innocence and compliance fool you.

241

Oh, no.

Is stubborness a trait of all Kazakhs? Frankly, I think, yes, it is. If you've been reading along with us on our journey, you may have sensed a wee bit of irritation on Heidi's part (not on mine, of course) with the Kazakh people. Whatever the case, these two little Kazakhs are stubborn beyond belief.

We have spent a lot of "quality time" with them, working on their little habit. Thankfully, Heidi and I are just as stubborn about simple obedience. Our best weapon is a short time out. Boy, do they hate having to sit still! We wonder, is it possible to be spoiled in an orphanage?! If so, these two have found the way.

We are all plodding steadily along, one step forward, and only 7/8th of a step back each day.

There have been a few catchphrases we've used on our journey: words we've written and said a number of times to help us get through.

"Leaf in a stream."

"Maybe, maybe not..."

"Eyes on the prize."

"Thank God, 24 is on!"

But the phrase we've said the most is by the wise philosopher, actor and comedian, William Murray. This adoption journey is all about one thing.

Baby steps.

HEIDI: These were difficult days for me. I really don't think Nik and Meg were purposely trying to misbehave. It's just that EVERYTHING was new to them. I imagine them thinking, "What will happen if I do *this*?" or "What if I try *that*?" All my Kazakh-proofing was not enough. It seemed that if I turned my attention away from them even for a second they'd be into something or other.

The baby home was not a place of fun and exploration. It was very regimented and buttoned down. Now Nik and Meg had a whole house to explore. What's okay and what's not? How do you know unless you try? And they tried. They tested the boundaries of everything!

MIKE: No one told me the days would be like this: continual kid correction. Showing them love by showing them boundaries. It really was exhausting. And discouraging. The days, even the hours, seemed endless. I think I could write pages, and it still wouldn't cover just how hard this time was.

How I wish someone who understood would have stopped by...told us that we weren't crazy; that all this trial and tribulation was normal. And, that it was okay to be frustrated and at your wit's end.

More than anything, my biggest complaint (and by now, you know I have a lot!) about this process was, we needed more support after we all got home.

If you know someone who has adopted…

I encourage you to encourage them! Your adopting friends are likely putting on a brave face. *After all, how could they not be happy, right?* Hopefully, you can see why they might not be. We received so much support along the way. However, we would have really benefited simply from words of encouragement during those dark days.

62. Joined at the Hip

Tuesday, October 12, 2004
Posted by Mike

It is important to realize that Meg and Heidi may never separate. Ever. I'm not kidding. You simply would not believe how that girl follows my wife around.

I've included a few pictures to give you an idea. It is pretty comical, really. We'll have a little fun and watch as Heidi moves from place to place. Meg tries to be all casual about it, looking the other way, pretending she's looking at the wall or something—until Heidi moves.

Then she'll ease ever-so-quietly toward Heidi, until she is a few inches away from her side. It's like a cartoon character trying to be nonchalant. All she needs to do is learn how to whistle as she sidles on over to where Heidi is. You have to laugh about it. Otherwise, Heidi would be going crazy by now. Just imagine what it must be like to have someone follow you everywhere you go.

244

All frickin' day. Every day.

Yes. Prayers are in order. For patience. And for speedy adjustments.

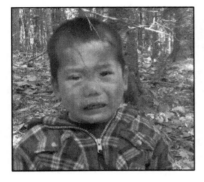

P.S. Let's not let Nik off the hook though. Here's a picture of him when we wanted to take a peaceful family walk in the woods...

Well, friends, we've come to the point in our journey where there just isn't too much exciting to write about! We've made it safely home, and all that's left is the tedious, tiring tasks of starting our new life together. If it's okay with you, we'll be "going dark" for awhile. Thanks so much for journeying with us. We made it! Keep us in your prayers and your thoughts and we'll post again when there's news.

HEIDI: It was not just Meg's proximity that was unnerving but how quiet she was about it. I wouldn't know she was even there until, by accident, I bumped into her or nearly knocked her over when I turned around or took a step.

To encourage parent/child bonding for the first several weeks, I fed Nik and Meg each and every meal. Feeding them also allowed me to control how much and how fast they ate. Of course I was concerned about choking but I was also concerned about overeating. They did not seem to know when they were full. I think if I'd let them, they would have just kept on eating and eating. It was a hands-on time, that's for sure.

We tried going to church. Nik and Meg did not understand the concept of "be quiet" or "be still" at all. Behavior and actions were unpredictable whenever we tried visiting family and friends and, if there were pets involved, forget it. They were terrified of all animals but especially dogs.

It didn't take long to see that "home" was enough to grasp and get used to. One area we focused on was teaching Nik and Meg how to interact with visitors who came into our home. At first when visitors came through the door (strangers to Nik and Meg, mind you), they would hold their hands, take their coats off, hug them, untie their shoes, and remove them. Can you imagine walking into someone's house only to have two tiny creatures practically pounce on you and proceed to take off your clothes? Most people thought this was so adorable and cute. I, on the other hand, was concerned. To me, this meant Nik and Meg had no fear of strangers. I can imagine this behavior might have been useful in the baby home but, in our culture, we want children to be wary of people they do not know. It took a long time to teach them not to open the door just because someone knocks. Better yet, don't open the door at all! Tell your mom or dad and let them open the door.

You may have noticed how all but the first post since my return was written by Mike. That's because every ounce of my time and attention was consumed with our new family. I had very little brain power to think, much less write. That's why it was decided a break from posting was in order.

MIKE: It was getting harder to think of positive, hopeful things to write about. We were exhausted from the adjustment. You can probably sense a bit of sarcasm (ok, more than a bit) in my posts. Those days taxed us to our limits, and beyond.

How do you write about the tedious in an interesting way? It was beyond my abilities. Several posts before, I wrote that our days were...

"...non-stop noise, dropping things, pooping, saying "No!" approximately infinity times, crying, wailing, stubbornness, sleeplessness, Kazakh ramblings, puzzled looks, pooping, poutings, and of course, pooping. It feels like forever (Maybe this is what Forever Family means?)"

That would remain the case for quite awhile.

In the next post, you see I made one final attempt to communicate. With much crying and wailing, we managed to get a family picture. And with much crying and wailing, Heidi and I managed to get it mailed out to our friends and family.

That about sums up the rest of the adoption year. I don't recall a lot of joy. But I do recall a weird sense of peace. We were making a small difference in the world. That kept us going. But make no mistake: it was a real challenge.

The Good Life: Plot

Once again, I'll comment on the necessity of the Plot Element for the Good Life. We all go through hard, trying times. When hope is in short supply, you've got to have a reason to keep going, something to remind yourself why it's worth it. Heidi and I had a plot for our family and our life. We clung to it like crazy. We couldn't have succeeded without it.

If you are adopting...

It's quite a challenging time, post-adoption.
Don't be afraid to ask for help. Be specific. Ask for a meal or an hour away. At the least, just *talk* to someone you trust.
Adoption. It'll test you to your limits. But you can get through it.
You *will* get through it. Trust me.
It's just gonna take awhile.

Keep your eyes on the prize. One baby step at a time.

63. A Happy Christmas To You!

Wednesday, December 8, 2004
Posted by Mike

If you're reading this, chances are you've received our Christmas picture. You may have noticed a few additional Vaydas of differing skin tone.

You've reached our blog chronicling just how we found these two. Please scroll back and read along on our journey. (You say you want a sneak preview? Difficult. Travel. Poop. Crying. Different language. Amazed.)

We wish you a peaceful, hopeful holiday season!

Mike, Heidi & the Vayda Family

MIKE: *What's funny about this Christmas picture is that Nik wouldn't stop crying and whining. We ruined a dozen shots. Finally, Grammie got him to smile...but by then, the other kids were grouchy and unsmiling. What to do?*

Get our good friend Lisa Horn to work her Photoshop magic! It's impossible to tell, but Nik's one smiling head was grafted onto this picture.

Thank you, Lisa. You saved our reputation as great parents!

64. One Final Conversation

NO ONE—ABSOLUTELY NO ONE—
IS GOING TO READ THIS.

Monday, February 14, 2005
Posted by Mike

When I was younger, I had visions of being a *Writer*. Kind of like Hemingway or Keats. Or John Boy Walton.

One of the side benefits of the adoption of Nik and Meg was that I was, for a brief time, a writer. I had an audience of people who looked forward to the story I was telling. I don't flatter myself too much here. I realize it was the story that was important, much more so than how I was telling it. Nevertheless, it was a great feeling to know that, as I posted the daily blog from Taraz, people were waiting to read it. From Maine to Ohio to Maryland to West Virginia to North Carolina and beyond, my words were being read. Pretty cool.

Then, I stopped writing.

Life just got in the way of writing *about* Life, I guess. Shortly after we got the kids home, it became very hard to find the time (or the words) to describe how things were going. We had these two strangers as part of our daily family living. I tried to keep the blog going. But, frankly, the drama was over. No more trips to a third world country, no more adventure and intrigue. Just the somewhat-mundane struggle to become a family.

I made one last gasp attempt at Christmas. I vowed to write something by the end of the year. But that didn't happen. It's now mid-February, for crying out loud. I don't even have a current picture. And, even though I realize the only person who will read this last post is me, I do feel compelled to finish. To end the current chapter of this new, lifelong story. But how best to end this blog?

My job entails quite a bit of traveling. This means dinner with clients. Inevitably, conversation turns around to our personal lives. We all miss our loved ones on the road, so we talk about them to feel closer. I'm a pretty private person, so very few people know our story of the past year. It's funny how a variation of the following conversation seems to always happen, every time I'm on the road.

I'll use this as a synopsis of "how things have been going" for us. Let's call this our little Adoption movie scene...

"An End to the Beginning"
INT. NIGHT: A nice restaurant in an unnamed city. At the table are five people on a business trip. Perhaps everyone is on to their second drink.

Associate 1: So, Mike! Do you have a family?

Mike: Yes, I do.

Associate 1: How many kids do you have?

Mike: Five.
(Stunned silence.)

Associates: F-five?

Mike: Yep. (More silence.)

Associate 2: What are their ages?

Mike: Well, let's see: Twelve, eight, seven, & two three year olds.

Associate 3: Oh! So you have twins?

Mike: No. (General puzzlement.) *The two little ones are adopted.*

Associate 1: Adopted? (A murmur ensues.)

Associate 2: Where are they from?

Mike: From a country called Kazakhstan. It's just south of Russia and west-ish of China.

Associate 4: Wow. What made you decide to do tha—um, I mean, why did you choose to adopt from there?

Mike: Well, my wife and I both wanted to adopt internationally. And Kazakhstan is known to take good care of its orphaned children. We always wanted our family to think outside our own culture. Plus, we think Asian kids are cute.

Associate 1: Uh huh...So, why did you decide to adopt in the first place? I mean, you already have three of your own...

Mike: Primarily because my wife made it a prerequisite to our getting married. I had to agree to it or she wouldn't marry me.
(General laughter to relieve the tension.)

Really, she's the one who kept the desire alive all these years. But I slowly began to see how adoption is a concrete way of living out what I believe. I want to make sure I make a difference for Good in life. This is one way to do that.

Associate 1: It's an awful huge commitment!

Mike: Yes. It is.

Associate 4: Well, how do your kids—I mean, your three, um, natural kids—I mean, older kids—feel about it?

Mike: Surprisingly good. At first there was resistance, which you'd expect. It was all about "How will this change things for me?" But, slowly, they began to buy into the concept of this being a family mission. By the time we left for the trip, they were on board 100%.

Associate 1: How long were you over there?

Mike: The first time, for a month.

Associate 3: A month! What was it like?

Mike: It was hard. It made us evaluate how committed we really were to this thing. For me? I remember looking at my wife the first day we were there. We were in this small hotel room, in a very foreign country, and realizing, all I have is her. That's all I know here. And it really cements your relationship. Looking back, we had a pretty good time, the two of us.

Associate 1: So you brought the kids back after that?

Mike: No. We came home for ten days, then Heidi went back a second time. This time, her mother went with her and I stayed home with the kids. They were gone for two more weeks. Then they came home with the kids.

Associate 2: Are the kids real brother and sister?

Mike: Not by blood. But they were both from the same baby home. So they knew each other.

Associate 1: How was it at first?

Mike: It was pretty hard the first few weeks. They were very stubborn and it takes time for them to learn what is acceptable in an orphanage is not in their new home. I imagine it's a bit like two families living together after a re-marriage—except for the Kazakh language thing.

Associate 3: You mean they didn't speak any English?

Mike: Nope.

Associate 2: Do you guys speak…Kazakhese?

Mike: Kazakh? None.

Associate 1: So…how did you communicate?

Mike: I remember lying in bed after we all got back to the US, thinking, What if there's an emergency? How can they tell us what's wrong? It's easy to get really freaked out. But all you can do is go forward in faith. The whole thing is a leap of faith.

Associate 2: So, what did you do then?

Mike: We just tried to communicate in any way we could. It's gotten a lot better now. Now they're reading Shakespeare to us at dinner.

(General laughter to lighten things.)

Associate 1: So, how are the older kids doing now?

Mike: I never thought I'd see those three be this unselfish. They're really helping a lot. I'm not sure we could've done it without them. It's no picnic but, overall, it's been positive for all the kids.

Associate 3: How does your wife do it when you're on the road like this?

Mike: God only knows. She's amazing. You'd have to ask her, but I think she'd tell you, you just keep going.

Associate 1: How long have they been home?

Mike: About five months now.

Associate 2: How are they adjusting?

Mike: I'd say great. They are very comfortable and seem to be having a blast. All of us are still a little freaked at being a family of seven. Especially when we're walking through the mall. But you kind of start accepting the stares with a bit of pride. It's not always a bad thing to stand out from the crowd. And we watch a lot of Brady Bunch reruns.

Associate 2: Do you two just sit there in tears at what you're doing? I mean, it's truly amazing.

Mike: No. Maybe a tear or two wishing the two of us could have just one quiet dinner like this one. But, really, you just do the best you can. And pray a lot.

Associate 3: What's the one thing you wish you had?

Mike: Alice. We really want Alice from The Brady Bunch to come live with us.

Shortly after that, the conversation moves on. Which is fine. I don't want to be known as "the adoption guy." But what is really cool is this: At some point during that discussion, you can see something happening to the people around the table. (This may sound a bit strange, but stick with me here.)

You can see each person changing while we're talking—at least for a moment. They are thinking about something other—something outside and above—their everyday life. They reconnect with the fact that Life is not really about business deals or sports or acquiring wealth or celebrity. They think about the way they're living it, the choices they're making—or not making. It doesn't last for long. But it happens every time.

For me? These moments are such an affirmation. I come home and tell my wife, *This* is why we're doing this. Not "just" for Nik and Meg. The choice we made, and are making daily, is having an impact for Good on everyone we talk to. Who knows how the story of Nik and Meg will effect a change in the life of a stranger, someone they never meet?

This adoption is the challenge of my life, thus far. But it's already rewarding me in rich and surprising ways.

Now if they could just pee in the potty.

HEIDI: Alice from *The Brady Bunch* never showed.

For me, I operated in something like a depressed, sleep-deprived fog for a long time. The truth is, although I did "just keep on going," everyday was really hard. Since my dream of adoption had finally become reality, I thought I should be constantly on cloud nine and it seemed like others expected me to be thrilled all the time, too. Instead, I mostly felt dull and without hope. There was such disparity between how I thought I should feel and how I actually felt.

Time alone was something I could only vaguely recall. The peeing and pooping never seemed to end. I was tired. As the stay-at-home mother, I was day and night trying to understand and integrate two toddler-aged non-English speaking strangers with three existing older siblings. I was trying to make sure every person in this new family was getting what they needed. *Was any progress being made?*

Gradually I noticed my outlook begin to improve as we neared the two-year mark. (You read that right.) The monotony of cleaning up mess after mess, potty training, and working on proper behaviors leading to temper tantrums day after day got the better of me sometimes. Emotionally those were dismal days for me.

But, slowly, I began to see the light at the end of the tunnel. Nik and Meg were eating and peeing and pooping on their own. We'd added a cute yellow lab named Rosie to our family. Within a few short weeks, Nik and Meg were playing with and loving the best dog ever. Familiarity with Rosie helped Nik and Meg overcome their fear of animals. This allowed us to get out to visit friends and family who had animals. I was seeing Nik and Meg's behaviors improving. They were not taking strangers' clothes off anymore! See, progress. They were acting more appropriately for longer periods of time. Life in our household was mostly manageable.

The Vayda family had begun their new life, together.

A question to consider
What examples can you see that Mike & Heidi were living in a "brave new world?" What does your brave new world look like? What proof do you have that you're living in it? If you're not there, what do you need to do to get there?

*(For more questions and your **free** study guide, go to **NotFar.org/Kaz**)*

Epilogue

15 years after

The first picture we ever received of Nik & Meg, April 2004

Nik & Meg's graduation day, May 2019

65. Where We are Now

HEIDI: It's been a journey of discovering who Nik and Meg are, from seeing them in that doorway all the way until...now. It's as though we have been putting together a puzzle with important pieces missing. Critical pieces, like family background and medical history, never arrived. There's so much information we've never been able to fill in on any school or medical form. Instead we must write, "history unknown, adopted."

As we raised Nik and Meg, we discovered more and more about them. It is an evolving process that has required adjustments to our hopes and expectations for them. Not always easy as a parent.

We have discovered a lot over the years. At first, Meg seemed to have developmental delays. Developmental delays became learning delays and, after struggling with processing and memory limitations, she was eventually diagnosed with an intellectual disability. This took years to uncover. Meg has a nurturing spirit and likes to help others, especially little children. She has an intuitive nature, an artistic and creative flair, and beautiful curly hair (when she doesn't decide to straighten it, like in the picture above).

Along the way, Nik developed allergies to cats and hay, and needs an inhaler now and again. For all the crying and wailing in the posts, Nik is actually a happy-go-lucky person who is easy to get along with. He likes to make people laugh (maybe too much, thus the reason for several parent/teacher conferences over the years!). He enjoys photography and videography, and has teaching and leadership skills.

There is a saying, "Anything worth having comes at a cost." Zack, Jake, Brynn, Nik, Meg, Mike, and I would not be who we are today but for adoption. It's not been easy but we added worth to our family when we chose adoption. Each of us in the Vayda family is a better person because of this choice.

MIKE: *A journey of mysteries. The entire adoption process, and these two children, are wonderful, miraculous brain teasers; whodunits without all the clues. The years since we left Maine for that crazy trip to Kazakhstan have been a slow unfolding of who these two strangers are.*

By now, we feel we know each other fairly well. I constantly forget to introduce them as my children, never realizing that, to outsiders, there's nothing to show that they are. Sure, they're Asian and I'm white, but, come on, can't you see the resemblance?!

Every so often, I'll look at one of them and wonder, how do they feel about being my child, really? About being Asian inside a White family? About never knowing their birth mother and father? When I ask them, they give me a quizzical look and shrug. Mysteries.

Eventually, we left Maine and moved to a college town in Ohio, and part of the reason was to be in a more culturally diverse environment. It was good for Nik and Meg to see Asian college students walking around town and to have more diversity in their own school. Our family was different now. All of us needed to see more colors and cultures!

Closer to the Good Life

We didn't just assimilate Nik and Meg into our family. That's what I thought would happen. Something better occurred; they also changed us. Because of the adoption, the course of the Vayda Family altered forever. By traveling to Kazakhstan, we became aware of a much bigger world outside middle class America. We never knew it was there! Once we woke up to this world, we knew: we needed to live differently.

A couple years after the adoption, Heidi and I went to India on a medical mission trip. We, of course, aren't doctors, but we wanted to learn about poverty, health issues, cultural barriers to living. We saw little babies of the poor and illiterate mothers, and we thought of Nik and Meg. These babies were dying from diseases the world already has the cures for! They were dying because the mothers lacked education.

We planned for a whole year. Then we went back to India and made videos for those mothers, so they would know how to care for their Niks and Megs (and Zacks, and Jakes, and Brynns). Those videos were used in many hospitals, and it made us feel good to know that those children would live and thrive.

Later that year, we started a nonprofit. We called it NotFar, because we wanted to get people closer to Good, and to use our skills as communicators to do so. We've traveled back to India many times; to South America and Africa as well, to make whatever impact that we could. (We took Zack, Jake and Brynn on some of the trips, too.)

Honestly, we never knew that this was the life we really wanted. We thought we were happy with our old one. It was only because we took the risks of KazMainea that our eyes were opened—and our hearts were changed—to go in a new direction.

We never would have taken these risks or forged this path if it wasn't for Nik and Meg. We changed their world. They changed ours.

As we write these words, Nik & Meg are graduating from high school. Soon, they both will be "adults." (I do question why becoming 18 suddenly qualifies you to be an adult, but that's a different story.) Nik and Meg will be starting their own lives, outside of our home. As their parents, we'll be taking a step back. We've spent 15 years with them. Protecting them, teaching them, loving them, and now, releasing them.

Early on in the blog, Heidi said something like, We cannot guarantee success for them. All we can do is give them a chance. By going to a Kazakhstan baby home, bumbling through a culture and a legal system we never understood, and bringing them into our American family, we gave them an opportunity. Not a destination. More like a launching place.

Who would they be now if they were still in Kazakhstan?

I think a lot about that. I believe, firmly, they would be living a much worse life. I believe Meg would be battling her way and Nik would be charming his way, trying to scratch out some sort of life. Both would be without ever having a family. Instead, thankfully, they grew up with a family. And love.

Still, though, as they begin their own journeys now, I worry and wonder for their future, like any father. But I also have hope, because I know we gave them a good beginning. And I take great comfort in believing that the same grace that carried us through all the travels of KazMainea will carry them as they begin the new journey of their own lives.

A Final Word from Heidi & Mike

We are so grateful to the many people who joined us on the KazMainea journey back in 2004. Some of the most important:

- Zack, Jake and Brynn, for being willing to accept the Vayda Family mission of adoption. Your lives were forever changed. You gave so much. Thank you for being our children.

- Amy & Peter Robbins, for watching Zack, Jake and Brynn while we were in Kazakhstan.

- Barbara & Roland Warren, Heidi's mother and father, for being our biggest adoption advocates and supporters.

- Melissa and Kevin, Mike's sister and brother-in-law, who cheered us on and embraced Nik and Meg as family.

- Lisa Horn, for magically keeping the business running.

- God, for the ongoing, magnificent moments of grace.

We wrote this book for you, dear reader. We pray it helps you to be a supporter of adoption and the good it offers to the world. And we hope that maybe you'll be inspired to find your own ways of doing good.

But most of all—first of all—this book is for you, Nik and Meg. Sadly, you'll never have a baby book. You'll never have videos of your birth, or your first steps, first words or first anything. But you have a family. And now you have *KazMainea*. Thank you for being our children.

Godspeed to you, Nikolas Sergazy and Meg Zhansaya. As you start your own wild and crazy journeys, never forget that Momma and Poppa went halfway around the world to find you and bring you home. We love you.

Mom & Dad

GET CLOSER
TO YOUR OWN GOOD LIFE!

It doesn't take an adoption to find the life of purpose and happiness you've always wanted. Let's find it together! There's lots more about adoption, the Vayda Family, and many free, awesome resources to start living the Good Life.

Go to **www.NotFar.org/Kaz**

Made in the USA
Coppell, TX
26 October 2021